THE U.S. ARMY
INFANTRYMAN
VIETNAM POCKET MANUAL

Edited by Chris McNab

CASEMATE
Philadelphia & Oxford

Published in the United States of America and
Great Britain in 2021 by
CASEMATE PUBLISHERS
1950 Lawrence Road, Havertown, PA 19083, USA
The Old Music Hall, 106–108 Cowley Road, Oxford OX4 1JE, UK

Introduction and chapter introductory texts by Chris McNab
© Casemate Publishers 2021

Hardback Edition: ISBN 978-1-63624-030-5
Digital Edition: ISBN 978-1-63624-031-2

A CIP record for this book is available from the British Library

Printed and bound in India by Replika Press Pvt. Ltd.

Typeset by Lapiz Digital Services.

For a complete list of Casemate titles, please contact:

CASEMATE PUBLISHERS (US)
Telephone (610) 853-9131
Fax (610) 853-9146
Email: casemate@casematepublishers.com
www.casematepublishers.com

CASEMATE PUBLISHERS (UK)
Telephone (01865) 241249
Fax (01865) 794449
Email: casemate-uk@casematepublishers.co.uk
www.casematepublishers.co.uk

The information in this book is reproduced for study only. The publisher assumes no
responsibility of liability of any damage incurred resulting from following any of the
instructions printed in this book.

The images used in this publication are taken from public domain U.S. military, Department
of Defense and governmental sources.

CONTENTS

INTRODUCTION

For the U.S. Army, the Vietnam War was not simply another conflict in its long and mighty military history. It was rather a cultural and tactical fracture—as painful as a real bone break—separating the Army of World War II from the modern force it is today. As the bare statistics of the conflict suggest, much of the weight of this dark period in American history was carried by the Army infantry. Between August 1964 and May 1975, just over 9 million U.S. military personnel served on active duty, 2.7 million of whom went to Vietnam. Of these, about 75 percent were non-combatants, while the remaining 25 percent were destined to experience the violence of frontline life. The bulk of these men, as they have been since the founding of the United States, were infantry.

The U.S. descent into the Vietnam War was initially a gradual warming rather than a sudden rush deployment. The first U.S. military advisors, mainly Special Forces soldiers and helicopter crews, arrived in South Vietnam in 1955. Their numbers would steadily increase, especially during the early 1960s when it became apparent that South Vietnam's political and military infrastructure was struggling to contain the indigenous communist insurgency, sponsored by Ho Chi Minh's Democratic Republic of Vietnam (DRV; North Vietnam) across the northern border. By 1962, the number of U.S. personnel in-country totaled about 11,000, with the lines now blurring between advisor and combatant. Then, in 1964, the passing of the Gulf of Tonkin Resolution by the U.S. Congress gave President Johnson the green light to make full deployments of regular U.S. armed forces to Vietnam. America was now at war.

In terms of the first major infantry deployment to Vietnam, the U.S. Marines led the way when the 9th Marine Expeditionary Brigade was landed around Da Nang on March 8, 1965. But the U.S. Army infantry arrived shortly thereafter, and in ever-increasing strength. Between May 1965 and November 1967, division-strength Army infantry deployments to South Vietnam included (in sequence) the 173rd Airborne Brigade, 1st Cavalry Division (Airmobile), 1st Infantry Division, 25th Infantry Division, 4th Infantry Division, 9th Infantry Division, AMERICAL Division, and the 101st Airborne Division. The manpower for such massive overseas movements was heavily supported by the Selective Service Act, which resulted in some 1.7 million U.S. citizens between the ages of 18 and 27 being drafted into the armed services between 1965 and 1973. The majority of the draftees went into the Army; in 1965, about 20 percent of the infantry consisted of draftees, but that figure hovered more around 70 percent by 1973 (although by that time the numbers of U.S. troops in South Vietnam were dramatically fewer). Because of the complex system of deferments and exemptions that applied to the draft, recruitment leaned significantly towards the poorer and less well educated (only 40 percent of eligible college graduates would be recruited), and with an average age of 19 years old.

Those young recruits, after weeks of basic training and an 18–20-hour flight, found themselves in South Vietnam, beginning their first day of a 365-day tour, every subsequent day ticked off towards their Date Eligible for Return from Overseas (DEROS). Most infantry veterans remember the sheer culture shock. Everything was different and extremely so—the terrain, the climate, wildlife, food, religion, language, customs, behaviors, the million nuances that make a foreign culture. In many ways, Vietnam could seem even stranger by virtue of life on the massive U.S. bases, formed by American industry to make a simulacrum of home. The U.S. Army's Vietnam HQ base at Long Binh, for example, had 3,500 buildings and 180 miles of road, its facilities including 81 basketball courts, 12 swimming pools, 3 football fields, a theatrical amphitheater, and numerous restaurants, PXs (Post Exchanges, essentially military shopping malls), intellectual groups, and social clubs. In post-war analysis, some experts think that the presence of such bases could actually accentuate the likelihood of post-traumatic stress disorder (PTSD); the transition, via a 30-minute helicopter ride, from firefight to steak barbecue was too jolting on the mind. In stark contrast to such rear-area bases, however, were the often-remote firebases and outposts scattered throughout the Vietnamese countryside. On these, living was far starker, with little in the way of creature comforts, plus the added disadvantage of being a natural and highly visible target for Viet Cong (VC) and North Vietnamese Army (NVA) forces.

The infantryman in Vietnam would have to adjust to an entirely new life, and a way of looking at the world around him. Amongst other things, a new lexicon signaled this shift. The infantry were now "Grunts," the VC insurgents were "Charlie," and operations through the contested hinterlands were expeditions into "Indian country." After some months, the seasoned infantry would refer to new arrivals as "FNGs"—F*****g New Guys—and those working in safe (or at least safer) rear-area jobs as "REMFs" (Rear-Echelon Motherf*****s).

Vietnam infantry veterans, reflecting on those wilder years, often remember the boredom and routines of base life or the occasional hedonistic batch of R&R. But it is the experience of combat that was most formative. Vietnam was a combat-intensive theater, being both an insurgency war (against the VC) and a conventional conflict (against the NVA). Depending on where they were posted, and the missions with which they were tasked, some infantry units might experience combat on some level for nearly every day they were deployed away from a major rear-area base. Drawing the roughest of historical lines, we can divide the combat history of U.S. forces in Vietnam into two major blocks. The first, from

1965 until the beginning of 1968, saw U.S. ground infantry (Army and Marines) primarily deployed in search-and-destroy (S&D), clearing, pacification, and security operations, as they attempted to find, fix, and destroy major VC and NVA forces in the South while also seeking to improve security against infiltration in civilian areas. This was a period of major S&D actions, involving thousands of troops, hundreds of helicopters, and a tactical focus on attrition—kill as many of the enemy as possible, and keep doing so until he folds. Then in January 1968, the NVA launched the Tet Offensive, a vast conventional offensive across the length and breadth of South Vietnam. It failed, at least tactically, but the scale of its shock to American politics and society led to President Richard Nixon (who took office in 1969) declaring the progressive and irrevocable withdrawal of U.S. troops from South Vietnam, transferring responsibility for the war effort to South Vietnam's own armed forces. Here began the second major period, known as "Vietnamization." U.S. Army infantry would, during this time, still perform major combat operations, some of these every bit as large as the missions of 1965–68. But by the end of 1973, all U.S. combat troops had been withdrawn from South Vietnam.

The experience of infantry combat in Vietnam was fluid. Much of the fighting was done at a small but harrowing scale, single-digit casualties clocked up regularly from ambushes and booby traps during patrols and village searches (the latter sometimes referred to as "Zippo missions," as they often resulted in U.S. troops burning down rural housing with their Zippo lighters). The Vietnam veteran and author Philip Caputo has remarked that while the casualties of such actions were limited, especially when compared to the mass dead and wound of infantry combat in World War II, the effect was that each fatal casualty died as an *individual* to those around him, driving the impact home mentally. There was the added confusion that it was frequently difficult, if not impossible, to distinguish between enemy civilian and combatant, leading to at best mental and verbal hostility towards civilians and at worst indiscriminate violence. Compounding the stress of combat, operations were also conducted under the worst that Vietnam's climate could throw at the young soldiers, not only scorching daytime temperatures and suffocating humidity, but also freezing winter temperatures on mountain peaks or blinding curtains of monsoon rains.

At the other end of the scale, however, were the major S&D actions, huge combined-arms maneuvers involving multiple battalions and complex airborne and overland deployments. Just one of many examples is Operation *Attleboro*, which ran from September 14 to November 25, 1966, in Binh Duong Province. This operation to destroy major VC and NVA base areas eventually became a corps-level operation, involving the 196th Light Infantry Brigade (who launched the operation), 1st Infantry Division, 4th Infantry Division, and 25th Infantry Division. The action resulted in ferocious and prolonged open battles with the division-strength NVA regular units. Using the attrition metric, the battle was a resounding U.S. success, with the NVA bases destroyed (at least for the time being) and more than 1,000 enemy killed for 155 U.S. dead and 5 missing. Other similar epic sweeps include Operation *Cedar Falls* (January 8 to 26, 1967) and Operation *Junction City* (February 22 to May 14, 1967), the latter using 249 helicopters to deliver one of the largest airborne assaults in history.

The experience of the U.S. Army infantryman in Vietnam, therefore, carried with it the most potent sensory, moral, and mortal impact. Many paid an ultimate price. In total, the United States lost 58,152 personnel killed in Vietnam, plus another 153,303 significantly wounded (serious enough to require hospital treatment). While the dead naturally attract our reverence, due consideration should be given to the wounded, as tens of thousands of American veterans would eventually return to a civilian life that now had to be adapted around one or more missing limbs, or other debilitating and life-long health conditions. Furthermore, taking the total casualty figures illustrates just how dangerous service was in Vietnam— one in ten Americans who went to Vietnam would be either killed or wounded. Although the U.S. Marine Corps took heavier casualties as a percentage of its Vietnam deployment (66,227 killed or wounded/22.5 percent), the Army suffered the largest volume of casualties overall: 134,982 killed or wounded (38,179 dead), which equates to 9.5 percent of its Vietnam force. To these casualty figures we can add the various estimates for those veterans suffering from PTSD. The estimates vary considerably in figures, from about 15 to 50 percent of veterans being afflicted. The actual number cannot be arrived at with any precision, but it is certainly another serious impact to be weighed.

This book explores the experience of the U.S. Army infantryman in Vietnam not through first-hand accounts, but through a selection of official textual sources. These sources include contemporary field manuals and technical manuals, infantry guidebooks, instructional booklets, weapons manuals, intelligence documents, after-action reports, and more. They have been selected from a truly vast archive— Vietnam was a massively documented conflict, the levels of paperwork and printouts partly generated by the U.S. military's age-old need to codify doctrines and record actions, partly through a political emphasis on applying management techniques to warfare, and partly through the rise of new digital means of recording and storing information. The result is a sprawling labyrinth of opinion, analysis, and planning. This book brings together sources that throw direct light onto the experience of the frontline infantryman in Vietnam, from adjusting to Vietnamese culture as a recruit fresh off the plane to operating a Claymore mine in an ambush. Although there can be some significant difference between reality and written records, taken together these sources provide a detailed insight into how the U.S. Army infantry was adapting to an emerging type of warfare—counterinsurgency—and doing so with a new generation of weapons and equipment.

CHAPTER I
TRAINING AND ORIENTATION

During the Vietnam War era, the process of turning a new recruit into combat-ready infantry typically took about 16 weeks, consisting of an eight-week Basic Training (BT) program followed by an additional eight weeks of Advanced Individual Training (AIT). These programs gave the soldier the fundamental tactical and procedural skills to operate as infantrymen. AIT also included a spell at *Tigerland*, the name of the semi-tropical U.S. Army training camp located at Fort Polk, Louisiana, which offered a swampy, hot, and vegetation-choked environment that was deemed approximate to the conditions experienced in Vietnam.

The American infantryman in Vietnam was essentially locked into two wars, that against the enemy and that against the climate and terrain. The most pervasive and inescapable problem for infantry on operations was Vietnam's elevated heat and humidity, which when combined with the physical exertion of patrolling or combat brought the perfect pressure-cooker conditions for heat exhaustion. During one infantry action in April 1967, for example, 60 men became heat exhaustion casualties in just the first three hours of the operation.

But Vietnam had other adverse weather effects, outside of the clammy heat. During the monsoon season (May–October), there could be rainfall of the most extraordinary volumes on a near daily basis. In one instance on October 5, 1969, the city of Hue received 22 inches of rain in just 24 hours. Outside the city, such rains turned the landscape into leg-sucking agonies of movement, while also rotting uniforms, equipment, weapons, and human skin.

The Vietnamese jungle, which covered large extents of the country, was not the only battleground for the U.S. infantry, but it was the most physically challenging. As FM 31-30, *Jungle Training and Operations* (1965), here explains, just moving through the jungle landscape was problematic, especially when trying to execute tactical maneuvers. Dense-packed vegetation could slow the pace of advance to a crawl while also wrapping itself around the infantryman in a claustrophobic experience. Any exposed skin would quickly receive small, easily infected cuts and puncture wounds from sharp grasses and thorns. Then there was the wildlife—leeches, spiders, biting flies and centipedes, venomous snakes, rats, even big cats. Worst of all were the mosquitoes, which attacked the soldiers in relentless clouds. One soldier remembered how, during the monsoon season, it was raining so hard that he was struggling to breath, so put his face down with his hands making a protective cup around his nose and mouth. Almost immediately, the space within his hands was entirely filled with mosquitoes. Aside from the discomfort, the mosquitoes also brought malaria, a major cause of non-battle casualties.

The first manual extract given is from FM 31-30. Although the American military had gained experience of jungle warfare in World War II, those memories were much faded by 1965 when this manual was written, and when the first major infantry deployments were sent to Vietnam

From FM 31-30 *Jungle Training and Operations* (1965)

CHAPTER 2
THE JUNGLE

Section III. MILITARY ASPECTS

17. General

Movement either by vehicle or on foot is extremely difficult in jungle areas. Minor terrain features can present major obstacles to movement in combination with the dense vegetation. Because bridging equipment generally will not be available at any depth in the jungle, it is necessary to improvise for almost every river crossing where fording is not possible. Planning criteria must first be developed on the time factors involved rather than the distance to be covered. Defensive action in jungle terrain is considerably aided by natural features. Small units are the essential element in all jungle operations. They must be kept fully informed of the known situation, so they can make competent plans and decisions.

18. Observation and Fields of Fire

a. Observation. Ground observers are at a distinct disadvantage in jungle areas. The range of horizontal visibility is extremely limited. Aerial observation will provide little useful information because the jungle canopy will conceal most activity underneath. This activity may include movement of substantial bodies of troops over fairly long distances. Undetected movements of this type can mean disaster if defending troops cannot properly man defensive positions before the attack. Conversely, the attacking forces may also use the jungle cover and concealment to get into positions undetected by and unknown to the defenders. In these areas of limited observation and fluid frontal conditions the control of the fighting becomes doubly difficult. Flanks can be turned, fronts can change, and the leaders of the operation may never know that these events have occurred.

b. Fields of Fire. The traditional employment of automatic weapons is impractical in jungle areas. It is not normally advisable to clear fan-shaped fields of fire to provide maximum arc and coverage of sectors with these weapons. To do this would indicate clearly to the enemy the friendly fields of fire. Rather, "fire tunnels" should be carefully hollowed out of the vegetation to define the sectors of fire. For the most part coverage will be limited to the control of trails and other routes of movement and fire will be confined to very shallow areas. Even the range for snipers will be very short. Short range, quick-burst, quick-response weapons are the most useful.

19. Concealment

In nearly all types of vegetation in jungle areas the concealment potential is tremendous. The opportunity to conceal troops from most types of surveillance devices is afforded in all types of vegetation except the very young secondary growth group. If camouflage techniques are used properly there are very few situations or conditions in which troops cannot be concealed from ground observers. Seasonal changes of coloration must be studied. Stringent discipline must be maintained in all movements and bivouacs to insure against unnecessary clearing of overhead cover and thereby permit aerial observation. Many of the vegetative features that afford concealment because of their opaque surfaces provide no resistance to bullets. It is easy for troops to mistake concealment for cover.

20. Cover

Except in the primary evergreen rainforest, the trees in most jungle areas will not provide extensive cover. Average tree trunks are generally not more than 12 inches in diameter; in areas where large trunked trees are located the trees are usually widely spaced. Most of the cover in jungle areas will be afforded by surface irregularities, such as ravines, gullies, and large rocks. These are to be found in abundance.

21. Obstacles

The jungle itself is the obstacle. This feature with its attendant psychological pitfalls and its physical adversities must be overcome before any thought can be given to an enemy force. The stresses placed on men to merely traverse the ground and the heat generated by such stresses induce a type of hypnotic spell in which the next step becomes the most important consideration, all of which dulls the mental discipline necessary to remain alert. Augmenting the natural conditions that serve to break down the spirit and fighting will of the soldier are the manmade obstacles erected by the enemy. If these obstacles are encountered when troops are in a state of fatigue they may forget that the obstacles are almost always controlled by maximum enemy firepower. Only a determined, disciplined force in peak physical condition can hope to move and fight successfully in the jungle.

22. Key Terrain Features

All features that expedite movement, resupply, and evacuation may be key terrain features. Roads are the most critical; trails that afford relatively easy access are next in priority. Navigable waterways are also significant. Any clearing in which a helicopter can load or unload may tactically be a key feature in a major operation. Villages, bridges and prepared fords must also be considered. Unlike conditions in more barren areas, high ground is not necessarily important; from the heights the possibility of controlling or observing trails or critical approaches through the valleys is rather remote.

23. Avenues and Routes of Approach

It is not possible to provide a formula for deciding the approach route that would serve the needs of the commander best. If he has a choice, his immediate needs and the time/ distance factor will guide him in his decision as to routes for movements. Consideration should be given to the fact that in any movement security is of major importance. Although the terrain may permit movement along trails, ridgelines and valleys, normally these routes will be guarded by enemy forces. On the other hand, while travel across ridgelines and valleys will normally offer more security, it will be much slower and extremely tiring for the troops, especially so if large quantities of food and ammunition are to be carried.

CHAPTER 3
JUNGLE TRAINING

Section I. THE INDIVIDUAL

24. General

A practical appraisal of the abnormal difficulties inherent in jungle operations will reveal that the only remedies for such conditions are training and experience. Unless, however, experience is based on sound, thorough, realistic and constant training it is liable to be quite costly. Therefore, the individual soldier and operational units should be prepared to live and fight in jungle environment before such a mission is actually assigned. Training conducted in actual jungle constitutes the ideal training situation; however, application of guidance herein described, in areas other than the jungle, will benefit the soldier, in the event jungle areas are not available. Under circumstances of the nonavailability of jungle terrain, commanders must employ vigorous and imaginative approaches to training for jungle combat taking advantage of the opportunities offered by dense woods, river beds, swamps, marshes or thickets for training purposes. Application of night fighting techniques when utilizing conventional or relatively barren terrain for training will prove to be quite effective in simulating the reduced ranges of assault, restricted movement, and control difficulties imposed by the jungle.

25. Initial Training Objectives

a. The first concern of commanders who are faced with the task of preparing individuals for jungle combat is the physical and mental acclimation of troops to the oppressive jungle environment. Psychological conditioning and knowledge imparted through sound instruction are the only means to eliminate the common fear of snakes, insects, animals, and unknown, foreboding terrain. Troops must not only be physically hardened; in addition, they must be able to adjust to weather, climate, and temperature changes to be expected when deployment to wet tropics from temperate areas takes place.

b. The objectives of jungle training are to prepare the individual and unit to function effectively in jungle environments. Training situations should be created which require execution of missions by small units operating independently. Control of units should be decentralized requiring reliance upon the junior leaders and even the individual soldier. Training should demand individual self-reliance, teamwork, skill, and determination on the part of participating troops. The scope of the training program should extend from survival of the individual in the jungle, to participation of units in combined operations.

26. Acclimation to Heat and Humidity

a. General. One of the secrets of successful training or fighting in a wet tropical climate is the knowledge and proper use of information regarding the acclimation process of the body, heat disorders, and basic heat rules. It must be emphasized that understanding and remembering this information are not enough; only by proper use of this knowledge can troops avoid becoming heat casualties.

b. Heat. Heat is a physical form of energy generated through combustion, chemical action, or friction. There are two types of heat which are of interest to the soldier, the heat of the environment caused by the sun, and the heat of the body generated by converting food into energy. The normal temperature of the human body is between 98° F and 99° F depending on the individual. When excess heat acquired by the body from the environment or from energy producing foods is not dissipated, and this internal temperature departs significantly from normal, serious sickness or even death will result. The human body dissipates excess heat in three ways: conduction, radiation, and evaporation. Conduction of body heat occurs when the temperature of the air is less than the body temperature. Radiation of body heat occurs when the surface temperature of surrounding objects is lower than the surface temperature of the skin. Normal responses to heat stresses are dilation (enlargement) of the blood vessels and an increase in the rate of heartbeat. These adjustments increase the temperature of the skin and thus increase heat loss through conduction. When radiation is not sufficient to maintain the normal body temperature, the activity of the sweat glands increases and evaporation of the perspiration from the surface of the skin becomes the most important means of cooling the body.

c. The acclimation process. Acclimation can be defined as the adaptation by the individual to work in the heat with maximum efficiency and least discomfort. If the body does not become accustomed to heat, the individual becomes irritable and sluggish and is unable to sleep. In general, the performance of this individual becomes substandard and inefficient. Some soldiers may never become acclimated but, fortunately, the percentage is very small. The acclimation process is automatic. The ease and rapidity with which the body becomes acclimated depends upon several variables. One such variable is the degree of temperature change between the two climates involved. Troops going to the wet tropics from a southerly location in the mid-latitudes will become acclimated easier and faster than troops from a place farther to the North. A similar condition would exist if such a move is made in the summer instead of the winter. A second variable is the abruptness of the change from one climate to another. Troops who are transported to wet tropical areas by surface transportation will not experience as much discomfort when they arrive as would troops who are transported by air.

(1) *Characteristics of the acclimation process.*

(a) Acclimation begins the first day of arrival in the wet tropics and is well developed by the fourth day.

(b) As the process continues, sweating increases and begins more readily, but salt loss becomes less.

(c) Physical exercise speeds the acclimation process by inducing profuse sweating.

(d) The body will remain acclimated from one to two weeks after departure from wet tropical environment.

(2) *Proper clothing for the acclimation process.*

(a) Clothing must fit loosely. Tightly fitted uniforms will become saturated with sweat and will hinder the cooling process of evaporation and air circulation around the body.

(b) One loose layer of clothing is the most effective dress for the jungle as it affords some protection from brambles and insects and allows rapid evaporation of sweat.

[...]

28. Living in the Jungle

a. General. It is essential that the individual soldier be conditioned to the peculiarities and the unique jungle environment before he is committed to actual combat in this type of terrain. If not properly acquainted with the jungle, troops are liable to become occupied solely with their surroundings and give little attention to the assigned mission. Troops must know how to protect themselves from the elements and difficulties of the jungle, if their fighting efficiency is to be maintained. This is best accomplished by practical survival training which emphasizes the importance of individual resourcefulness, imagination, and determination. The soldier should acquire and apply sound habits to the everyday routine of living when operating in the jungle for extended periods. Jungle operations require independent actions by small units. As a consequence, the soldier must be prepared to care for his own needs.

b. Aspects Affecting Troops Living in the Jungle.

(1) *Individual uniforms, clothing, and equipment.* Troops conducting jungle operations will usually have to manpack their essentials as normal methods of logistical support will not usually be available. Therefore, each soldier must learn what his requirements for clothing and equipment are, how to keep these requirements to a minimum, and how best to use them.

(a). Combat uniform (fatigues). This clothing is adequate, as issued, for wear in the jungle. To insure maximum cooling of the body, ventilation, must carry away body heat. The fatigues, therefore, must fit loosely; they should not be "cut-down" or tailored. To aid ventilation, troops should be allowed to wear the jacket on the outside of the trousers. To take advantage of the blending color of the fatigues with the background offered by the jungle, the clothing should not be excessively faded from the original olive green color. Faded and light colored fatigues will outline the wearer's form against the jungle green. Fatigue clothing should also be in serviceable condition. Worn or threadbare cloth will not protect the soldier from insect bites, brambles, and direct sunlight as well as new or heavy cloth. The skin needs all the protection it can be given. Troops should not depend upon a uniform that may tear easily and expose areas of the body.

(b) Poncho. The poncho is a raincoat and is issued as such. However, if the poncho is worn as a raincoat its nonporous structure will cause perspiration and will cause the soldier to be more uncomfortable, and wetter, than he would be if he did not attempt to clothe himself against the rain. Also, the vegetation will literally tear the poncho from the wearer's body. By employing the poncho as an expedient it will be found that it has many more useful purposes that will serve troops better. The poncho is very useful in the construction of shelters. […] The poncho can also be used to gather rain water, as an improvised parachute for material drops and for the construction of brush rafts.

(c) The jungle boot. It is light weight and has built-in drainage screens located at the inside arch. These two features aid swimming while wearing the boots.

An outstanding advantage offered by the boot is its cleated sole, which aids in negotiating steep slopes and ground covered with wet and decaying vegetation. If jungle boots are not available, cleated soles should be provided on the standard combat boot.

(d) The insect (mosquito) bar. The mosquito bar is a most important item of equipment. Although it is very light it can be bulky if not folded carefully. For efficient packing the mosquito bar should be folded inside the poncho, the roll being as tight as possible. This roll can then be fastened onto the top of the combat pack with straps, or attached to the suspender harness with light rope if the pack is not worn. The mosquito bar should be utilized whenever troops sleep in the jungle. If conditions prevent construction of a shelter the bar can still be used by tying to trees or brush. Besides providing protection from insects, the mosquito bar will offer protection from bats, whose bites are a potential source of rabies. One word of caution. Troops should not allow any portion of the body to contact the mosquito bar when it is hung, as mosquitos and bats will bite through the net.

(e) Gloves. If available soldiers should wear gloves when moving through vegetation. Some protection from thorns, brambles, insect bites, and snake bite will thus be afforded. Gloves will also protect the hands from blisters when using the machete for prolonged periods of time and will prevent burns when rappelling rapidly. When not actually needed, they should not be worn, because they will soften the skin unnecessarily.

(f) Suspenders. The suspenders issued with the combat pack should be worn when the accouterment belt is worn. Because it is advantageous to travel light, troops should not wear the combat pack except when the mission dictates. As much as possible, individual equipment and ammunition should be worn on the belt. The suspenders will help support the weight by relieving weight from the hips and, as a result, the load will be easier to carry, being better distributed.

(g) The machete. The machete is the most important and useful piece of equipment available to the jungle fighter. It is an effective weapon as well as an excellent cutting tool. The employment of the machete as a weapon can be integrated with other combat training. As a tool, however, the machete shows its worth. To gain the maximum use from the machete, it is necessary to learn and practice the proper grip. The proper way to grasp the machete is as follows: take a firm grip on the handle, the power of the grip being asserted by the thumb, the index finger and the third finger; the ring finger and the small finger should be held loosely around the handle; the last two fingers will be tightened around the handle immediately prior to the blade striking the target. Simultaneous with this last action a pronounced "snap" of the wrist will be made. This will increase the power of the strike. To realize the

maximum efficiency of the blade, the angle of strike should be 45°. Caution should be exercised to insure that the blade does not strike the target at an angle greater than 45° as the blade will make only a shallow cut. If the target is struck at an angle less than 45°, the tendency is to ricochet. Besides being ineffective, this is very dangerous to the wielder of the machete and to those around him. The machete is also used to cut grass. However, when the machete is employed to do this, repeated blows may be necessary to cut one clump of grass. This is caused by the resiliency of the grass and the resultant lack of resistance offered to the blade. A simple expedient can solve this difficulty. A forked stick will compress the grass so that the blade will cut it. This stick will also flush away from the user's immediate vicinity any snakes that might be there. Certain precautions must be taken when troops use the machete. Users should not cut towards the body; they should swing the blade away to the left or right. In cutting vines, when making a trail, the cut should always be upward to avoid jerking the tree tops to which the vine

PITCHED CANOPY FASHION

Hasty shelter constructed with the poncho.

is fastened, and thus alerting any enemy observation. Individuals should not work too closely to one another. The back of the blade is thin and can injure, so care should be exercised when the blade is drawn back in preparation for a strike. When not in use the machete should be sheathed. If it must be carried unsheathed, it should be grasped by the back of the blade between the thumb and the index and third fingers. Thus, if a soldier should fall the blade will be dropped and the reflexive action of extending the arms to break the fall will not result in injury. Like any other tool, the machete must be properly maintained.

The relationship between American servicemen and Vietnamese civilians defies easy explanation, as it stretches across such extremes of behavior. At one end of the spectrum, there was the undoubted engagement of tens of thousands of soldiers in the battle for "hearts and minds," striking up good relations with local people. These might express themselves in culture-bridging formal activities, such as providing security for villages or participating in infrastructure projects. Often they might be more specific and personal, such as a growing friendship or even a romantic involvement. (Tens of thousands of Amerasian children were born in Vietnam during the years of U.S. deployment, although given the prevalence of desperation prostitution many of these children were not necessarily the result of a thoughtful relationship.)

Yet at the other end of the spectrum was the hatred and violence towards South Vietnamese civilians, most chillingly represented by the My Lai massacre of March 16, 1968, when as many as 500 unarmed Vietnamese civilians were killed by U.S. Army soldiers from Company C, 1st Battalion, 20th Infantry Regiment and Company B, 4th Battalion, 3rd Infantry Regiment, 11th Brigade, 23rd (*Americal*) Infantry Division. Many veterans acknowledge that the blurred lines between VC fighters and regular civilians could breed hatred and a callous indifference to the fate of civilians.

A Pocket Guide to Vietnam (1962) was issued to most U.S. soldiers heading out to service in South Vietnam. Its purpose was to help the American warrior make a respectful attempt to understand a people and country that were utterly unlike anything else back home. We should remember that in these days before common international tourism, most American soldiers would have never been out of their own country. The first time they did so, unfortunately, was to step into a war.

From *A Pocket Guide to Vietnam* (1962)

AT HOME WITH THE VIETNAMESE

You will find many areas of common interest with the Vietnamese: their regard for their families … their historic struggle for national independence … their wish to allow people individual freedom within the framework of laws made for the good of all.

But there are many differences between their culture and customs and our own and you must be prepared to deal with them in a way that will make you an acceptable friend of the Vietnamese.

Some of the differences are small things, like the way a Vietnamese seems to be waving goodbye when he is actually beckoning you to come toward him. You should not use typical American motions to beckon Vietnamese as they use such gestures only for animals. Also do not slap a man on the back unless you know him very well.

More important differences are attitudes toward older people, manual labor, display of emotion, and time. For instance, the average Vietnamese is less compulsive about time than the American, and you should not consider it a personal affront if people arrive late for an appointment or even if they don't arrive at all.

Moderation should be practiced in all things and the moral code of the people you are among strictly observed. Knowing that trouble breeds in situations where a person has one drink too many or forgets to show the utmost respect and courtesy toward women, you should make it a special point to avoid getting even close to the fringes of this sort of trouble. Never interfere in an argument among Vietnamese. A good general rule is to avoid all incidents that do not concern you directly.

Family Loyalty

The Vietnamese are justifiably proud of their culture and national identity, but their primary social outlook revolves around their family and village. These claim first allegiance. Members of a family, for instance, have an absolute obligation – to be violated only at the risk of serious dishonor – to care for their relatives and to prevent any of them from being in want. Even after a girl marries, her love and respect for her parents traditionally continue to overshadow her love and respect for her husband.

The traditional family unit includes living and dead members and members not yet born. On festival days and in family ceremonies the ancestors are revered, and at all times there is thought of the grandsons and great-grandsons yet to be born who will carry on the family name. A family without male heirs is assumed to have disappeared.

The importance of family is evident in the many terms used to denote family relationships. In addition to the usual ones like father, mother, brother, sister, the Vietnamese have terms to show relative age, the father's side of the family versus the mother's, and other niceties of relationship. In keeping with the lesser importance of younger people, there is only one term for a younger brother or sister. Either is *em.* but *anh* means elder brother and *chi,* elder sister.

Older people with their accumulation of a lifetime of experience are considered the wisest members of society and therefore are accorded the highest standing. If you are invited to a Vietnamese home for a meal, be sure to let the older people begin eating before you do. Be solicitous about helping them to things on the table. Older Vietnamese, by the way, will usually not shake hands but will greet you by joining their hands in from of them and inclining their heads very slightly. Responding with the same gesture will show them that you know and appreciate this respectful custom.

Woman's Place Is at Home

Since the purpose of marriage is to continue the family line, the parents believe that the selection of a proper wife for their son is their personal responsibility, a duty they owe both to their ancestors and to their son and his future children. Usually with the help of a "go-between," they search for a girl who is skillful at housework and who will be a good mother to many children. Beauty is not as desirable as good character. In fact, beauty is sometimes considered a disadvantage because the Vietnamese believe that fate seldom is kind to beautiful women.

The traditional position of women is totally subordinate to men and their social life is limited. At the same time, wives often exercise a great deal of influence in the family, particularly in connection with financial affairs and, of course, in selecting marriage partners for their sons and daughters.

People of upper-class families, as well as people living in villages removed from big city and Western influences, continue to follow time-honored traditions and customs. Among others, the customs have been considerably modified. Women are assuming a new and important position in the life of the nation, and young men and women are breaking away from traditions to choose their own marriage partners.

The Professional Man

The Vietnamese have always felt that a deep division exists between manual and "intellectual" labor. Traditionally Vietnamese who have achieved positions with the Government as a result of long and patient study, or who have become doctors, teachers, and so on, avoid using their hands for tasks they feel they have graduated beyond. It would be unusual, for example, to see such a person washing his car, helping his wife clear the table, or working in the garden.

Another thing, a Vietnamese might avoid looking a superior in the eye when talking to him. This does not mean the man cannot be trusted. It means he is being polite by not "staring" at a person of greater standing.

At your first meeting with a Vietnamese he might ask: "How much money do you make?" This is a natural question in the sequence of "Are you married?" and "How many children do you have?" It simply expresses polite interest. If you feel uncomfortable about replying, you can avoid a direct answer by stating that you are paid in American dollars and don't know what the equivalent would be in Vietnamese currency. Your indirect reply lets the other person know you do not want to answer and have told him so politely. The matter is thus dropped without embarrassing anybody.

If you want to ask a favor, you should remember that hinting and indirection are preferable to making an outright request. Also avoid launching too quickly into a new topic or disagreeing too vehemently. Exercise moderation in your conversation. At a first meeting, it is often best to stay on topics like families or the weather.

Politeness and Restraint

Even among the most sophisticated Vietnamese, manners have not become lax or social customs unrestricted. Manners are conditioned by age-old religious teachings and are deeply ingrained in the life of the people.

Public display of emotion is almost always considered in bad taste. Raising the voice, shouting, or gesturing wildly are most impolite. Tied in with the view that marriage is primarily for continuance of the family line is a feeling that display of affection should be confined to the privacy of the home – and even there, not practiced before guest.

The Vietnamese regard men and women who walk arm-in-arm as vulgar. But you may occasionally see two boys or men walking down the street hand-in-hand. This is an ordinary mark of friendship common to many Asian and other countries.

If you follow the general practices of good manners and courtesy, and observe those that are particularly important to your Vietnamese hosts, you will be a welcome guest in Vietnam. This is vital to your mission there. You will fulfil your duty at all times that you are in a land where dignity, restraint, and politeness are highly regarded.

Town and Country

The architecture of homes in the cities and towns shows French and other Western influence, and decoration and furnishings also have a decidedly Western touch. But in the rural districts and mountain villages you will find thatched roofs, mud walls, pounded dirt floors, and little furniture. Some of the more pretentious rural houses have tile roofs, wooden walls, and floors of tile or flat brick squares set in mortar.

A feature of most homes is the family altar containing a tablet bearing the names of the family's ancestors going back at least to the great-grandfather. Veneration for the family's ancestors is perpetuated through the eldest son who is expected to succeed his father in caring for the altar. The altar may take up as much as one-sixth of the entire floor space of the house, excluding the kitchen. The kitchen is customarily built adjoining but separate from the living quarters.

Another interesting feature of a Vietnamese home is the plank bed. Often made of costly wood with inlaid mother-of-pearl, the bed may be as large as eight by five feet. Except for a mosquito net there is generally no bedding. The Vietnamese feel that in their hot climate it is more comfortable to sleep without bedding.

Village Life

The Vietnamese village, *lang* and *xa,* is an administrative unit rather like a county in the United States. It is made up of a number of scattered hamlets or *ap,* each set against a backdrop of bamboo thickets and groves of areca (betel nut) and coconut palms. Located as the village seat of government are a school, athletic or parade field, and a meeting hall. Some villages also have a dispensary and a maternity building containing a couple of beds and staffed by a trained midwife.

An "information" booth displays Government notices. Saigon newspapers may be kept here for public reference. The *dinh*, or village communal temple, houses a decree naming the village guardian spirit.

There is also a village market. On market day, which is once or twice a week, people file out of the hamlets to follow the narrow paths or rice paddy banks to the marketplace. They come to sell, to buy, or just to gossip. Some balance baskets of fresh fruits and vegetables on their heads.

A shopper can buy live chickens or duck eggs, conical hats to ward off the sun and plastic coats to keep away the rain, or Chinese herbs and Western aspirin, and even a brightly colored scarf in which to carry purchases.

A popular feature at the market is the man with a portable stove-and-bakery suspended from the ends of a bamboo pole balanced across his shoulders. From this ingenious double-duty device the merchant offers noodle soup on one side, papaya and red peppers on the other.

Men of the 2nd Platoon, Company "C," 2nd Battalion, 60th Infantry, 9th Infantry Division, pass a Vietnamese hut during an operation in the Plain of Reeds, 9 April 1968.

What's for Supper?

The average Vietnamese consumes less than two-thirds the calories the average American puts away every day. Starvation is extremely rare, but the basically vegetarian diet sometimes lacks proteins, vitamins, and minerals.

Most middle-class families have ample meals consisting of four types of food: one salted, one fried or roasted, a vegetable soup, and rice. The soup (*canh*) is an important part of the meal and may contain bits of fish or meat along with the vegetables.

Rice is the staple food and its preparation is a grave responsibility for the women of the household. All girls are supposed to learn to cook as an essential part of their education. During the Moon Festival they prepare their best dishes so that the eligible bachelors may see how well they can cook – particularly *banh trung chu* – the special Moon Festival Cakes.

CHAPTER 2
EQUIPMENT AND WEAPONRY

In every aspect, the materiel superiority of the armed forces of the United States in the 1960s and 1970s was unassailable when compared to the more modest resources of its opponent, North Vietnam. The United States was the world's greatest superpower, by a long margin, whereas North Vietnam was still effectively a developing nation, albeit one sponsored by China and the world's other superpower, the Soviet Union.

The American superiority was particularly marked in naval assets, airpower, logistics, artillery, communications, and surveillance. Down at the frontline infantry level, however, the advantages were somewhat ironed out. Certainly, the U.S. infantryman in Vietnam could often draw on formidable support fire, and his kit and equipment would be of better quality and availability, but small-unit actions were still largely decided by small-arms and hand-deployed explosives, and especially by the rifle each soldier carried. This rifle, for most soldiers in Vietnam, would be one of Eugene Stoner's M16 family, which was new on the scene. It represented something of a revolution in U.S. infantry standard-issue firepower. Unlike the wood-and-steel full-caliber rifle powerhouses of the past, the M1 Garand and M14, the M16 was built heavily of lightweight aluminum and plastics and fired a small but high-velocity 5.56 × 45mm round either in semi-auto or full-auto modes. Its first iteration, from 1962, was the XM16E1, then came an improved version, the M16A1, in 1965, carried by the infantryman through the rest of the war.

The two following sources focus heavily on keeping the M16 functioning. This was not just a matter of sound practice. In its first years of use, the XM16E1 gathered caustic criticisms for being fundamentally unreliable, with combat malfunctions resulting in the deaths of some U.S. servicemen and much suspicion about its value. Ultimately, the problem was found to lie more in poor propellant rather than the gun itself, but in both sources here the urgency of keeping a clean gun is apparent.

From FM 23-9, *Rifle, 5.56-mm, XM16E1* (1966)

11. Maintenance

a. General. A clean, properly oiled and maintained rifle loaded with clean ammunition will shoot when needed. In order to keep the M16Al rifle and ammunition in good condition they must have daily care and cleaning. Under bad weather conditions certain key parts of the rifle and ammunition may need care and cleaning several times a day. To insure proper functioning of the M16A1 rifle, it is imperative that the following procedures be followed:

b. Cleaning. Thoroughly clean all metal surfaces of the rifle with bore cleaner (solvent cleaning compound, CR). Special attention must be given to the following areas in order of their importance to functioning:

(1) *Chamber.* Clean the chamber with a chamber brush dipped in bore cleaner. Wipe with clean dry swabs (cleaning patches) and apply a light coat of LSA (lubricating oil, semifluid, MIL-L- 46000A).

(2) *Bolt carrier group.*

(a) Carrier key. Clean the bolt carrier key with a bore brush dipped in bore cleaner. A used or worn brush should be used if available. Wipe with a clean, dry pipe cleaner (FSN 9920-292-9946).

(b) Locking lugs. Clean the locking lugs of the bolt, extractor and extractor well using a small brush and bore cleaner. Remove any accumulation of dirt, carbon or oil from the firing pin, the external and internal surfaces of the bolt and bolt carrier using a small brush and bore cleaner. Also clean the firing pin hole of the bolt using a pipe cleaner soaked with bore cleaner. Wipe all parts with a clean dry swab, rag or pipe cleaner. Apply a generous coat of LSA to the exterior surfaces of the bolt carrier, a light coat of LSA on the bolt, interior of the bolt carrier and one drop of LSA in the carrier key.

(c) *Magazine.* Must be disassembled and wiped clean with a clean, dry rag. Lightly oil the magazine spring only by wiping with a rag dipped in LSA.

(d) *Barrel bore.*

1. Attach a bore brush to an assembled cleaning rod, dip in bore cleaner, and brush the bore thoroughly. Brush the bore from chamber to muzzle using straight through strokes.

Note. Do not reverse direction of brush while in the bore. Push the brush through the bore until it extends beyond the muzzle. Continue until the bore is well covered with bore cleaner. Remove the brush from the cleaning rod, attach the slotted tip, and dry the bore by pushing through clean dry swabs. Continue until swabs come out clean and dry. Care should be used to support the cleaning rod while inserting to prevent flexing or breakage.

2. After cleaning, lubricate the bore with a lightly oiled swab to prevent rust and pitting. Lightly oil the lugs in the barrel extension.

(e) *Upper receiver.*

1. Use a swab or brush to clean the upper receiver of powder fouling with bore cleaner.

2. Clean the protruding gas tube in the receiver with a worn bore brush attached to a section of cleaning rod. The top of the gas tube can be cleaned by inserting the rod and brush in the back of the receiver. The sides and bottom of the gas tube can be cleaned from the bottom of the receiver.

3. Wipe all parts dry.

4. Apply a generous coat of LSA to the interior surfaces of the upper receiver.

(f) *Lower receiver.*

1. Cleaning will not require detailed disassembly of the lower receiver group. Using a swab or bristle brush with bore cleaner, remove carbon, dirt and sand from the lower receiver. Dry and generously lubricate with LSA.

2. After extensive use, acids caused by perspiration should be removed from exterior surfaces using a rag or swab with bore cleaner, then wipe dry and apply a light coat of LSA.

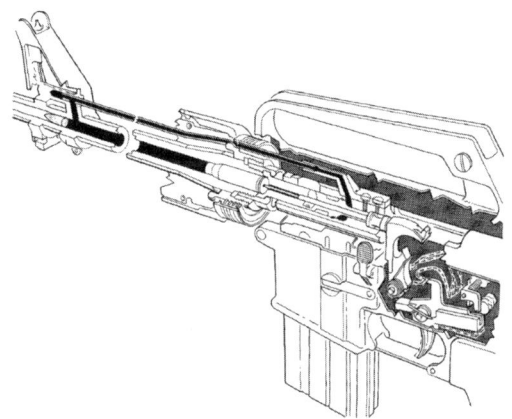

XM16E1 internal action on firing.

From "M16 Rifle Tips" (1967)

The M16 is the finest military rifle ever made. It's lightweight, easy to handle, and will put out a lot of lead. If you know it, respect it, and treat it right, it will be ready when you need it. The following tips are from combat veterans who wanted to pass on to you their ideas on weapon care. Learn 'em, use 'em, and you'll not be caught short!

a. Keep your ammo and magazine as clean and dry as possible. Lightly lube the magazine spring only. Oil it up, and you're headed for trouble.

b. Inspect your ammo when you load the magazines. Don't load dented or dirty ammo. Remember, load only 18 or 19 rounds.

c. Clean your rifle every chance you get. 3–5 times a day will not be too often in some cases. Cleanliness is next to godliness, boy, and it may save your life.

d. Be sure to clean carbon and dirt from those barrel locking lugs. Pipe cleaners help here and in the gas port.

e. Don't be bashful about asking for cleaning materials when you need 'em. They're available; get 'em and use 'em.

f. Check your extractor and spring often; if they are worn or burred, get new ones ASAP.

g. Lube your rifle using only LSA. That's the best. A light coat put on with a rag after cleaning is good. Functional parts need generous applications often. Put a very light coat of LSA in the bore and chamber after cleaning.

Officially, U.S. infantry rifle platoons of the Vietnam era were organized into a three-man HQ, three 10-man rifle squads, plus an 11-man weapons squad, the latter including two M60 machine guns (each with a two-man crew) and two M67 90mm recoilless rifles. The M60 would be the standard platoon and squad support machine gun of the Vietnam War. When the platoon came under fire, each machine-gun team could quickly drop down, set the gun firmly on its bipod, and start running through belts of 7.62 × 51mm ammunition at a cyclic rate of 650rpm (maximum practical rate was more in the region of 100rpm). The bullet of the M60 had far greater range and penetration than that of the M16, so was ideal for punching through thick foliage and enemy cover. It could be an awkward weapon to use, however, being heavy to carry and with a problematic barrel-change system, two reasons why the gun was affectionately known to troops as the "Pig." Note that in Vietnam the realities of (low) unit strength and tactics often changed the organization of the platoon and rifle squad; the latter could creep as high as 12 men, and might include one or two M60s of its own.

From FM 23-67, *Machinegun, 7.62-mm*, M60 (1964)

2. Roles of the Machinegun

The machinegun supports the rifleman in both the attack and defense. The machinegun is capable of engaging distant targets with a heavy volume of controlled and accurate fire that is beyond the capability of individual weapons. It provides the rifleman with the heavy volume of close and continuous fire necessary to accomplish his mission in the attack. The long range, close defensive, and final protective fires delivered by this weapon form an integral part of the unit's defensive fires.

3. Description

a. General. The M60 machinegun is an aircooled, belt-fed, gas-operated automatic weapon. The weapon fires from the open-bolt position. Ammunition is fed into the gun by a disintegrating metallic split-link belt. Two barrels are issued with each weapon. The weapon features fixed headspace which permits rapid changing of barrels.

b. Sights. The M60 has a front sight permanently affixed to the barrel. The rear sight leaf is mounted on a spring-type dovetail base. It can be folded forward to the horizontal when the gun is to be moved. The range plate on the sight leaf is marked for each 100 meters, from 300 meters, to the maximum effective range of 1,100 meters. Range changes may be made by using either the slide release or the elevating knob. The slide release is used for making major changes in elevation. The elevating knob is used for fine adjustments, such as during zeroing. Four clicks on the elevating knob equal a 1-mil change of elevation. The sight is adjustable for windage five mils right and left of zero. The windage knob is located on the left side of the sight. One click on the windage knob equals a 1-mil change of deflection.

c. Safety. A safety lever is located on the left side of the trigger housing. It has an S (SAFE) and an F (FIRE) position. On the SAFE position the bolt cannot be pulled to the rear or released to go forward. The cocking handle, on the right side of the gun, is used to pull the bolt to the rear. IT MUST BE RETURNED MANUALLY TO ITS FORWARD POSITION EACH TIME THE BOLT IS MANUALLY PULLED TO THE REAR.

d. Flash Suppressor. A flash suppressor is affixed to the muzzle of the barrel. The ribs of this suppressor vibrate during firing and dissipate flash and smoke.

e. Bipod Mount. The M60 can be effectively fired from the integral bipod mount. The hinged shoulder rest provides support for the rear of the gun. The movable carrying handle provides a method for carrying the gun short distances and can be positioned out of the gunner's line of sight.

f. Tripod Mount. The M122 tripod mount provides a stable and durable mount for the M60 machinegun. Firing the gun from a tripod permits a high degree of accuracy and control.

[…]

Section III. FIRE CONTROL

71. General

a. Fire control includes all actions of the leader and crew(s) that are connected with the preparation for and application of effective fire on a target. It is the ability to select and designate targets for the appropriate gun(s), open fire at the instant desired, adjust the fire of the gun(s), regulate the rate of fire, shift from one target to another, and cease fire.

b. Ability to exercise fire control depends primarily on the ability of the leader and the discipline and training of the crew. Failure to exercise fire control results in ineffective employment of the machinegun and can result in danger to friendly troops, loss of surprise effect, premature disclosure of positions, fire on unimportant targets, loss of time in adjusting fire, and a waste of ammunition.

72. Methods of Fire Control

There are several methods of controlling machinegun fire. The noise and confusion of battle will limit the use of some of these methods; therefore, the leader must select the best method or combination of methods which will best accomplish his purpose.

a. Oral. This is an effective method of control; but at times, the leader will be too far away from the gun crew(s) or the noise of battle will make it impossible for the gun crew(s) to hear him.

b. Arm-and-Hand Signals. This is an effective method when the gun crew(s) can see the leader. All crew members must understand the standard arm-and-hand signals [...]

c. Prearrange Signals. These are either visual or sound signals such as pyrotechnics or blasts on a whistle. These signals should be included in appropriate SOPs and must be clearly understood by all crew members.

d. Personal Contact. In many situations. the leader must move to individual crew members to issue orders. This method of control is used more than any other by small unit leaders. The leader must use maximum cover and concealment to keep from disclosing the gun crew's position.

M60 machine gun team in action, 1966.

e. Standing Operating Procedures. Standing operating procedures are actions the gun crews perform automatically without command. SOPs […] are developed during the training of the gun crews, and their application eliminates many commands and simplifies the leader's job of fire control.

73. Fire Commands

a. When the leader decides to deliver fire on a target which is not obvious to the gunners, he must give them the information they will need to place effective fire on the target. He must get their attention, tell them what the target is, where it is located, which rate of fire to use, and give the command to open fire.

b. A fire command is given in order to accomplish this quickly and without confusion. Fire commands are either initial or subsequent. Initial fire commands are issued to begin firing at a target, and subsequent fire commands are issued to adjust fire, change the rate of fire, interrupt fire, shift fire to a new target, or to terminate the alert.

c. The noise and confusion of combat, and the separation of the guns make the use of complete fire commands, particularly oral commands, difficult and impractical. Therefore, abbreviated, informal fire commands (initial and subsequent) are more appropriate. However, before the crew members can react properly when they receive informal or abbreviated fire commands, they must have a complete understanding of the standardized fire command.

The Claymore mine was one of the most formidable defensive weapons available to the U.S. Army infantry squad in Vietnam. Effectively it was an explosive ball-bearing thrower, with devastating antipersonnel effects over a wide arc. Typically, Claymores would be set up for perimeter defense, either tripwire detonated or command-detonated by the human operator. At night, they might also be used alongside M49A1 trip flares, which could also be rigged to a tripwire and when activated would ignite a magnesium flare burning at 50,000 candlepower for up to 70 seconds. Claymores were much in use in Vietnam, with consumption of the mines at one point running at 80,000 per month.

From FM 23-23, *Antipersonnel Mine M18A1 and M18 (Claymore)* (1966)

CHAPTER 1
INTRODUCTION

[…]

Section II. DESCRIPTION

3. General

The M18A1 antipersonnel mine was standardized in 1960, and replaced the M18 antipersonnel mine. Both mines are similar in appearance and functioning. The M18A1 is a directional, fixed-fragmentation mine. When employed in the controlled role, it is treated as a one-shot weapon. It is primarily designed for use against massed infantry attacks; however, its fragments are also effective against light vehicles. The M18A1 mine is equipped with a fixer plastic slit-type sight (knife-edge sight on later model), adjustable legs, and two detonator wells. The mine and all its accessories are carried in the M7 bandoleer. An instruction sheet for the M18A1 is attached to the inside cover of the bandoleer. […]

4. Casualty Effects

When detonated, the M18A1 mine will deliver spherical steel fragments over a 60° fan-shaped pattern that is 2 meters high and 50 meters wide at a range of 50 meters. These fragments are moderately effective up to a range of 100 meters and can travel up to 250 meters forward of the mine. The optimum effective range (the range at which the most desirable balance is achieved between lethality and area coverage) is 50 meters.

5. Danger Area

a. Danger From Fragments. The danger area consists of a 180° fan with a radius of 250 meters centered in the direction of aim.

b. Danger Area of Backblast and Secondary Missiles. Within an area of 16 meters to the rear and sides of the mine, backblast can cause injury by concussion (ruptured eardrums) and create a secondary missile hazard.

(1) Friendly troops are prohibited to the rear and sides of the mine within a radius of 16 meters.

(2) The minimum safe operating distance from the mine is 16 meters. At this distance, and regardless of how the mine is employed, the operator should be in a foxhole, behind cover, or lying prone in a depression. The operator and all friendly troops within 100 meters of the mine must take cover to prevent being injured by flying secondary objects such as sticks, stones, and pebbles.

CHAPTER 2
MECHANICAL TRAINING

Section I. INTRODUCTION

6. General

This section describes and illustrates the M18A1 antipersonnel mine and the electric and nonelectric firing systems that can be used to detonate the mine.

7. Detailed Description

a. Mine.

(1) *Nomenclature.* Mine, antipersonnel, M18A1.

(2) *Common name.* CLAYMORE.

(3) *Type.* Antipersonnel.

(4) *Weight.* 3½ pounds.

(5) *Dimensions.* 8½ inches long; $1^3/_8$ inches wide; 3¼ inches high (legs folded); 6¾ inches high (legs unfolded).

(6) *Firing unit construction.* The outer surface of the mine is a curved, rectangular, olive-drab, molded case of fiberglass-filled polystyrene (plastic). In the front portion of the case is a fragmentation face containing steel spheres embedded in a plastic matrix. The back portion of the case behind the matrix contains a layer of explosive.

(7) *Explosive*. 1½ pounds of composition C4.

(8) *Detonator wells*. Two detonator wells are located on the top of the mine which allows for single or dual priming. These wells are sealed by the plug ends of the shipping plug priming-adapters which prevent entry of foreign materials into the detonator wells. The slotted end of the shipping plug priming-adapter is used to hold an electric blasting cap in place when the mine is armed. The shipping plug priming-adapter is merely reversed when the mine is to be armed.

(9) *Peepsight and arrows*. The molded slit-type peepsight (or knife-edge sight) and arrows located on top of the mine are used to aim the mine.

(10) *Legs*. Two pairs of scissors-type folding legs located on the bottom of the mine enable it to be emplaced on the ground. The mine can also be tied to posts, trees, etc.

b. Accessories.

(1) *M57 firing device.*

(*a*) One M57 electrical firing device is issued with each M18A1. This device is a hand-held pulse generator. A squeeze of the handle produces a double (one positive, one negative) 3-volt electric pulse of sufficient energy to fire the electric blasting cap through the 100 feet of firing wire which is issued with the mine. The M57 device is 4 inches long, approximately 1½ inches wide, 3¼ inches high, and weighs three-fourths of a pound. On one end of the firing device is a rubber connecting plug with a dust cover. […]

(*b*) The safety bail on the M57 electrical firing device has two positions. In the upper SAFE position, it acts as a block between the firing handle and the pulse generator. In the lower FIRE position, it is clear of the firing handle and allows the pulse generator to be activated. […]

(*c*) The M57 electrical firing device and firing wire should not be discarded after initial use. Another electric blasting cap can be attached to the firing wire and the M57 device can be used to fire other devices, such as fougasse bombs and demolition charges, provided no more than 100 feet of firing wire and one M6 blasting cap are used.

(2) *M4 electric blasting cap*. The M4 electric blasting cap assembly consists of an M6 electric blasting cap attached to 100 feet of firing wire. Attached to the firing wire connection is a combination shorting plug and dust cover. The shorting plug prevents accidental functioning of the blasting cap by static electricity; the dust cover prevents dirt and moisture from entering the connector. The firing wire is wrapped around a flat paper and then rolled to

form a package 6 inches long, 4 inches wide, and 2 inches high. A piece of insulating tape is used to hold the package together.

Note. With mines of later manufacture, the M4 electrical blasting cap assembly is wound on a spool.

(3) *M40 test set.* The M40 test set is an instrument used for checking the continuity of the initiating circuit of the mine. [...]

Note. Only one of the six bandoleers in each packing box contains a test set. The bandoleer containing the test set is marked by an identification tag on the carrying strap.

c. M7 Bandoleer. The M7 bandoleer is constructed of water resistant canvas (olive-drab color) and has snap fasteners which secure the flap. The bandoleer has two pockets; one pocket contains the mine and the other contains a firing device, a test set, and an electric blasting cap assembly. A 2-inch wide web strap, which is used as a shoulder carrying strap, is sewn to the bag. An instruction sheet is sewn to the inside flap.

Section II. COVERAGE AND METHODS OF FIRE

8. Fire Discipline

Since the M18A1 mine can be fired only once, fire discipline is of paramount importance. The mine should not be used against single personnel targets; rather, it should be used for its intended purpose – massed personnel. When lead elements of an enemy formation approach within 20 to 30 meters of the mine, it should be detonated. If practicable, and to insure fire discipline, actual authority and responsibility for target selection and timely detonation should rest with squad leaders or their superiors.

9. Controlled Frontal Coverage

a. For effective coverage of the entire front of a position, mines can be placed in a line no closer than 5 meters and no farther apart than 45 meters. Preferred lateral and rearward separation distance is 25 meters.

b. If mines are placed in depth (from front to rear), the minimum rearward separation distance is 5 meters, provided secondary missiles are removed. This distance is sufficient to prevent possible disturbance or damage to the rearward mines.

10. Methods of Fire

The M18A1 mine can be employed in either the controlled or uncontrolled role.

a. Controlled Role. The mine is detonated by the operator as the forward edge of the enemy approaches a point within the killing zone (20 to 30 meters) where maximum casualties can be inflicted. Controlled detonation may be accomplished by use of either an electrical or nonelectrical firing system. When mines are employed in the controlled role, they are treated the same as individual weapons and are reported for inclusion in the unit fire plan. They are not reported as mines; however, the emplacing unit must insure that the mines are either removed, detonated, or turned over to a relieving unit.

b. Uncontrolled Role. Uncontrolled firing is accomplished when the mine is installed in such a manner as to cause an unsuspecting enemy to detonate the mine. Mines employed in this manner must be reported and recorded as land mines.

Section III. FUNCTIONING AND INSTALLATION

11. Functioning

a. Electrical Firing. When the M18A1 is armed, actuating the M57 firing device handle with the safety bail in the FIRE position provides sufficient electrical energy to detonate the M6 electric blasting cap. The detonation of the blasting cap, in turn, sets off the high explosive charge (composition C4). Detonation of the high explosive charge causes fragmentation of the plastic matrix and projects spherical steel fragments outward in a fan-shaped pattern. This mine is sufficiently waterproof to function satisfactorily after having been submerged in salt or fresh water for 2 hours.

b. Nonelectrical Firing. The M18Al mine is deliberately detonated by the operator pulling or cutting a trip wire attached to a nonelectrical firing device. A nonelectric blasting cap attached to the firing device and crimped to a length of detonating cord sets off the detonating cord. At the other end of the detonating cord, a second crimped nonelectric blasting cap, which is inserted in one of the detonator wells, detonates the mine.

12. Installation for Electrical Firing

a. Laying and Aiming.

(1) *Laying*

(*a*) Check to see that the mine and all accessories are in the bandoleer. Read the instruction sheet attached inside the bandoleer cover before installing the mine.

(*b*) Remove the electrical firing wire leaving the mine and other accessories in the bandoleer.

Warning: During installation the M57 firing device must be kept in the possession of the man installing the mine to prevent accidental firing by a second man.

(c) Secure the shorting plug end of the firing wire at the firing position. Place the bandoleer on your shoulder and unroll the firing wire to the position selected for emplacing the mine.

Note. The instructor sheet which accompanies the M18A1 mine with slit-type peepsight indicates that the firing wire can be unrolled from the mine or from the firing position; however, the firing wire should always be laid from the firing position to the mine emplacement.

(d) Remove the mine from the bandoleer; turn the legs rearward and then downward. Spread each pair of legs about 45 degrees. One leg should protrude to the front and one to the rear of the mine. Position the mine with the surface marked "FRONT TOWARD ENEMY" and the arrows on top of the mine pointing in the direction of the enemy or the desired area of fire. On snow or extremely soft ground the bandoleer may be spread beneath the mine for support.

(e) To prevent tipping in windy areas or when the legs cannot be pressed into the ground, spread the legs to the maximum (about 180°) so that the legs are to the front and rear of the mine. [...]

(2) *Aiming.*

(a) Mines with slit-type peepsight.

1. Select an aiming point that is about 50 meters (150 feet) to the front of the mine and about 2½ meters (8 feet) above the ground.

2. Position the eye about 15 centimeters (6 inches) to the rear of the sight. Aim the mine by sighting through the peepsight. The groove of the sight should be in line with the aiming point. The aiming point should be in the center of the desired area of coverage, and the bottom edge of the peepsight should be parallel to the ground that is to be covered with the fragment spray.

(b) Mines with knife-edge sight.

1. Select an aiming point at ground level that is about 50 meters (150 feet) to the front the mine.

2. Position the eye about 15 centimeters (6 inches) to the rear of the sight. Aim the mine by aligning the two edges of the sight with the aiming point.

An emplaced M18A1 Claymore mine.

[…]

14. Camouflage

a. Although the M18A1 is painted olive-drab to facilitate camouflaging, it is necessary to blend the mine into its surroundings to prevent its detection.

b. Only lightweight foliage, such as leaves and grass should be used to avoid increasing the secondary missile hazard to the rear of the mine.

c. Both the front and rear of the mine should be camouflaged with foliage. The firing wire should also be camouflaged or buried underground. If used, detonating cord should not be buried; however, it may be covered with light foliage.

The infantryman of the Vietnam War was a beast of burden. On a typical patrol, each soldier might be "humping" a total equipment load of about 65lb in weight, but often much more. The nature of the combat in Vietnam—in which minor enemy contacts might spiral out into a major prolonged engagement with uncertain short-term resupply—meant that many infantrymen went into action lugging far more than the official requirements. For example, the standard M16 rifle load was deemed to be 180 rounds, in nine 20-round magazines. (The 30-round magazines used today in the M16 had yet to be developed.) In Vietnam, however, the cautious infantryman might supplement his standard ammo with two or three canvas ammo bandoliers, each holding another five or six 20-round magazines. Similarly with water. Instead of a single one-quart canteen, the soldier would often take four to six quarts. Add grenades, flares, Claymores, M60 ammo, demolitions, comms, rations, and personal items, and the infantry might end up lumbering around like spacemen on the Moon.

Two main load-carrying systems were used by the soldiers in Vietnam: the M1956 Individual Load-Carrying Equipment (ILCE) and the M1967 Modernized Load-Carrying Equipment (MLCE). The latter was developed specifically for use in Southeast Asia, substituting the ICLE's cotton with nylon and using aluminum and plastic for as many fittings as possible. It was issued from 1968. Even with modern material advances, however, Vietnam's climate was especially hard on kit and equipment, and FM 21-15, *Care and Use of Individual Equipment*, provided advice on care and maintenance. Although this particular manual is dated 1977, two years after the end of the Vietnam War, it is little changed from manual advice given during the conflict, plus usefully incorporates the lessons learned in-country.

From FM 21-15, *Care and Use of Individual Equipment* (1977)

CHAPTER 2
GENERAL CARE AND MAINTENANCE

[...]

BOOTS, SHOES, AND INSOLES

A new pair of boots or shoes should fit you properly when new (TM 10-228); you should not expect them to stretch. Because boots and shoes should have a chance to air between wearings, wear one pair one day and another pair the next. Wear the ventilating plastic insoles so that air can circulate underneath your feet.

- **Cleaning and Drying.** Scrape dirt or mud from boots or shoes with a flat stick, brush, or dull instrument which will not cut leather or rubber. Using a small handbrush, wash the boots or shoes with mild soap and very little water. Remove all soapsuds, and wipe the insides dry with a clean cloth. Stuff paper in the toes while the boots or shoes are still wet to keep the leather from shrinking out of shape. Dry the boots or shoes slowly in a warm, dry place. **Do not dry by exposure to hot sun, fire, or other strong heat,** because this may damage the rubber or leather. Rubbing saddle soap into the boots or shoes before they are completely dry will help soften the leather. Wash the ventilating insoles with a warm solution of mild soap or detergent, and let them air-dry. **Do not boil the insole.**

- **Polishing.** Use only stains and polishes that match the color of the boots or shoes.
- **Repairing.** The direct molded sole (DMS) boots and shoes are nonrepairable, except for the heels, which may be replaced. You should have the heels replaced after wear of seven-sixteenths of an inch or more.

CANVAS EQUIPMENT

- **Cleaning.** Clean soiled canvas items, such as bags and packs, by dipping them vigorously in a pail of warm water containing soap or detergent. This prolongs the life of the item and prevents discoloration. If soiled spots remain after washing, scrub with a white or colorfast cloth, using warm soapy water or detergent solution. **Do not use chlorine bleaches, yellow issue soap, cleaning fluids, or dyes which will discolor the**

Fighting Load (left) and Existence Load (right).

item. Dry canvas items in the shade or indoors. **Do not dry them in the sun** because direct sunlight will discolor them.

NOTE: Certain canvas items, such as the carrier for the field protective mask and the small arms ammunition case, may be provided with fiberboard or plastic stiffeners. If so, clean these cases with a damp, soft brush and cool water only.

- **Repairing.** Repair small rips and tears as soon as you find them by following one of the procedures described at the beginning.

WEB EQUIPMENT

Clean web equipment the same way you clean canvas equipment.

Do not use chlorine, yellow issue soap, clothing fluids, or dyes.

Rinse all soap carefully from web equipment after washing, and stretch the item back to its original shape while it dries. Dry the equipment in the shade or indoors; *never in direct sunlight.*

Do not launder or dry webbing in commercial or home-type automatic laundry equipment. Do not attempt to dye web equipment or to repair it.

- If it is damaged, turn it in for repair or replacement.

NETTING

Wash netting with a solution of warm water and mild soap or detergent. Repair small tears and holes by placing pieces of adhesive tape or waterproof tape over both sides of each hole while the netting is flattened out. **Do not draw and tie the edges of the hole together, except in an emergency.**

FASTENERS

- **Snap Fasteners.** Be careful when you open snap fasteners. Place your thumb and forefinger between the two layers of cloth close to the fastener, then pry the ball and socket halves of the fastener apart. Do not tug at the cloth.
- **Slide Fasteners.** Even though slide fasteners (zippers) are of sturdy construction, they must be used *carefully*. When a slide fastener snags, do not yank or tug at it. Check the fastener; if a fold of fabric is pinched between the two halves of the track, unzip the fastener about an inch, smooth out the fabric, and try again. When the slide fastener works stiffly, rub a thin coating of wax or lead-pencil graphite on each side of the track, and work the fastener back and forth a few times. The wax or

graphite will lubricate the fastener and allow it to open and close more easily. Close the fastener before washing the garment.

- **Hook-and-Pile Fasteners.** The hook-and-pile fastener is used as a closure for equipment and clothing. It is made up of two sections of tape. One section contains many small nylon hooks; the other section is a woven pile with many small nylon loops. When the two sections are pressed together, the loops on the pile tape are engaged by the hooks on the hook tape, resulting in a tight closure. The closure is opened by firmly pulling one tape section from the other. Clean the fastener by washing or brushing, as necessary.

COATED ITEMS

- **Cleaning.** *Do not machine wash, machine dry, hot press, or hot iron coated items.* Wipe soiled coated items with a clean cloth, shampoo by hand with a soft bristle brush using warm water and a mild soap or synthetic detergent, and rinse thoroughly. Air-dry the items; *do not use direct heat as it will cause coated material to dry out and crack.*

  Make sure that such things as oil, grease, acid, or insect repellent are washed off as soon as possible.

- **Storing.** Store coated items as described earlier.

MESS GEAR

Your mess gear consists of the *messkit pan and the field mess knife, fork, and spoon.* Before using your mess gear, clean and dip it in boiling water for at least 3 seconds. **Eating with mess gear on which grease or food particles have been left may cause serious illness or make the food less appetizing.** After eating, food particles should be completely scraped off as soon as possible.

Clean mess gear by dipping it in a hot soap, detergent, or hand dishwashing solution (130°F). Use a brush, if you have one, to wash off food or grease; rinse thoroughly for about 30 seconds in clean boiling water. Air-dry the gear by swinging it back and forth until it is thoroughly dry. *Never wipe mess gear with a cloth or towel.*

CANTEEN AND CUP

Your plastic (polyethylene) water canteen holds 1 quart. The olive-drab canteen, which fits into the standard metal canteen cup, has a plastic screwcap with an attaching strap and is carried in the standard canteen cover. Wash the canteen and cup with warm, soapy water and rinse thoroughly; keep them drained and dry when not in use.

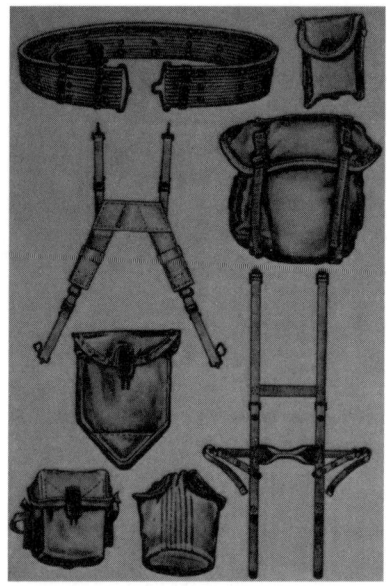

Components of the M1956 Individual Load-Carrying Equipment.

- Do not force the cap on the canteen; the plastic cap may split if not used properly.

When required, replace the cap with the M-1 drinking device; this device allows you to drink water from the canteen while you are wearing a protective mask.

NOTE: **Do not put the plastic canteen near an open flame or burner plate.**

MISCELLANEOUS EQUIPMENT

- **Sunglasses.** Wipe your sunglasses with a material that will not scratch the lens. To prevent sunglasses from becoming scratched or broken, put them in their case and pack them next to clothing or other soft material.

- **Pocketknife.** Clean your pocketknife often. The metal carrying ring attached to it is large enough to slip over the handle of the messkit pan so that the knife can be easily sterilized in boiling water. Sharpen the knife with a sharpening stone when possible. Dry the blades after each use, and oil the hinges and springs once in a while.

CHAPTER 3
CLOTHING

[…]

ARMOR VEST

- *Description.* The ballistic nylon armor vest has a lightweight, nylon cloth cover. The cover has two bellows patch pockets with flaps, and front hook-and-pile fastener with a flap covering, elastic side laces, and grenade hangers above each front pocket. The vest has a three-quarter, ballistic nylon collar.

- *Design.* The vest consists of a ballistic nylon filler which includes layers of tough nylon cloth stitched together to form the fragment-protective portion of the vest. A vinyl-plastic envelope covers the ballistic nylon filler, and this in turn is enclosed in a lightweight nylon cloth cover. The vinyl-plastic envelope forms a waterproof barrier against damage from moisture, dirt, and other foreign matter. The lightweight, nylon cloth cover provides camouflage, wear resistance, and added protection for inner parts of the vest. The cover has pockets and grenade hangers.

- *Fitting.* The chart below indicates the size vest you should select based on your chest measurements. Adjust the side laces so that the webbing strips with the lace eyelets touch, or butt, each other. If the vest is not comfortable, have someone loosen or tighten the elastic laces on each side. Check the fit while you are bending, stooping, and kneeling.

Armor Vest Sizes	
If your chest measures—	Select size—
36 ½" or less	Small
37"–40½"	Medium
41"–44½"	Large
45" or more	Extra Large

- *Wear.* Wear the armor vest for training or combat missions. When you wear it properly, the vest will protect certain vital areas against low-velocity mine, grenade, mortar shell, and artillery fragments, which cause most combat casualties.

The vest does not, however, protect against small-arms fire.

It does tend to decrease the severity of wounds from rifles and machineguns. Wear the armor vest with any type of combat clothing, and…

wear it at all times when you are within range of enemy weapons.

Wear the vest as indicated with the following uniforms or ensembles:

- *Utility (field) uniform and hot weather ensemble.* Wear the vest over your shirt or coat and under any additional layers of clothing.
- *Cold-wet ensemble.* Wear the vest over your field shirt and under the field coat with liner.
- *Cold-dry ensemble.* Wear the vest over the field shirt and under the field coat with liner or the parka with liner.

- *Inspection.* Examine your vest often for –
    - Tears, punctures, or damages to the outer nylon cover.
    - Bunching, caused by lumps or distortion in the ballistic nylon filler. Bunching is the creasing and folding of the nylon filler within the outer case.
    - Noticeable increase in weight, indicating the nylon filler has become wet.
    - Damaged or dirty hook-and-pile fastener.
    - Broken or missing elastic laces.

- *Care.* Keep your armor vest clean and in usable condition and it will protect you longer. If you do not wear it properly, it may result in less protection, and less protection may result in needless injury.

Do not use the vest as a seat cushion or a pillow. Careless handling and use of the vest for purposes other than body protection may damage the vest or may cause the protective nylon filler to bunch and leave you with unprotected areas.

- *Repairing.* Turn in a damaged vest as soon as possible. Until it is possible to turn it in, you can make certain temporary repairs. When the outer cover shows damage, first check to see whether the inner vinyl-plastic envelope has been damaged. If so, cover the damaged portion of the envelope with waterproof tape to prevent moisture from reaching the ballistic layers. Next, repair the outer nylon cover with tape to prevent further damage. When bunching occurs, try to remove it by inserting your hands through the vest armholes, lifting the vest, and shaking the ballistic layers back into position. Then smooth the whole area with your hands.

- *Cleaning.* Clean your vest regularly to prolong its protective life. **Do not use cleaning solvents or gasoline.** Hand-wash the vest by first removing the laces, brushing off mud and loose dirt, and then washing and rinsing it. *Be sure to wash and dry the front, back, and inside.* After washing, air-dry the vest, keeping it **away from direct heat and open flame.**

- *Storing.* Store the armor vest as follows:

  - Clean the vest thoroughly.
  - Clean the hook-and-pile fastener, untie the elastic laces, unlace the front and rear duck webbing, and open the side flaps.
  - Places the vest in a box, a carton, or open bin located inside a building or tent.
  - Cover the vest with a cloth or plastic sheet to keep out dust, dirt, and moisture.
  - **Do not fold the vest.**

GROUND TROOPS HELMET, CHINSTRAP, LINER, AND CAMOUFLAGE COVER

Helmet

- *Use.* Wear the ground troops helmet over the helmet liner for protection against ballistic-type fragmentation (such as that from artillery fire and grenades) and for protection against ricocheting bullets. The helmet and liner may be worn over the cotton utility cap or over the poncho hood.

- *Care.* Although the helmet is a sturdy item that can withstand rough treatment, you should not use it as a cooking pan; heat destroys the temper of the metal, weakens the helmet, and reduces its protective qualities. Also, do not use the helmet as a seat or as a shovel or hammer.

CHAPTER 5
LOAD-CARRYING RULES

[…]

ASSEMBLY FOR WEARING PACK ON SHOULDERS

The procedure for assembling the individual load-carrying equipment for carrying the field pack on your shoulders is described below.

1. **Adjust Belt.**

Adjust the belt the same as that for wearing the pack on the belt.

2. **Attach Suspenders to Belt.**

   FIRST…

   - Lay the belt out flat with the back facing up and the male belt fastener to your left, and locate the center eyelet of the belt.

   SECOND…

   - Attach the back suspender straps to the belt, one on each side of the center eyelet, by fastening the hooks on the straps to the top row of eyelets in the belt. Fasten the hooks from the inside to the outside of the belt.

   THIRD…

   - Attach the front suspender straps to the belt by fastening the hooks on the straps to the eyelets nearest the belt fasteners at each end of the belt.

3. **Adjust Suspender Straps.**

   - Put on the assembled belt and suspenders, and adjust the front suspender straps so that the belt is properly located at your waist. Then remove the equipment, and adjust the length of the back suspender straps so that the belt is even in the front and the back.

4. **Attach Ammunition Cases, First Aid Case, Intrenching Tool Carrier, and Canteen Cover to Belt.**

   - These items are attached the same as when you wear the pack on the belt.

5. **Attach Suspenders to Field Pack.**

   FIRST…

   - Attach the two snaphooks on the shoulders at the back of the suspenders into the eyelets of the two web tabs located on the field pack.

   SECOND…

   - Unfasten the two snaphooks of the back suspender straps from the belt eyelets.

THIRD…

- Pass the snaphooks and back straps through the two web loops on the field pack, and refasten the strap hooks into the belt eyelets.

6. **Attach Bayonet or Bayonet-Knife Scabbard, Hand grenades, and Sleeping Bag Carrier.**

- These items are attached the same as when you wear the pack on the belt.

7. **Attach Sleeping Equipment to Pack.**

- If the sleeping equipment roll is small, attach it directly to the bottom of the field pack, with or without the sleeping equipment carrier, by using the pack straps.

CARRY OF FIELD PROTECTIVE MASK

The recommended positions for carrying the field protective mask with the load-carrying equipment are as follows:

- The side-carry, with the shoulder strap over your right shoulder, the carrier and mask under your left arm, with the top of the mask placed in your armpit area; and the body strap fastened around your body.

- The leg-carry position, with the shoulder strap used as a waist strap, and the waist strap used as a leg strap.

[…]

Miscellaneous Information.

- The individual load-carrying equipment is designed so that it will balance with your equipment belt open. This design makes it possible for you to have ventilation by opening your equipment belt while on the march.

- Attaching clips, sliding keepers, hooks and buckles must be kept free of dirt to insure proper operation of the equipment.

- The load-carrying equipment is **not** fire resistant. It can be quickly damaged by sparks from open fires or by drying it too close to a hot stove. Take special care, therefore, to protect the equipment from sparks and to dry it slowly.

CHAPTER 3
UNDERSTANDING THE ENEMY

The U.S. infantryman faced against two main oppositional forces—the Viet Cong (VC) and the People's Army of Vietnam (PAVN), the latter also known amongst the Americans as the North Vietnamese Army (NVA). In many ways it was the fusion of these two enemies—one a highly developed in-country counterinsurgency force, the other a conventional army making regular and on occasions massive forays across the border—that made the Vietnam War so challenging for the United States, both tactically and strategically.

"Viet Cong" was actually American shorthand for the personnel of the People's Liberation Armed Forces (PLAF), the combat wing of the broader communist National Liberation Front of Southern Vietnam (NLF), although in its loosest expression "VC" could be applied to the total NLF organization. The VC was no amateur guerrilla force. It was large (245,000 strong by the end of 1967), well-organized, and highly motivated, and included battalion- and regimental-strength units capable of conventional operations. The VC combatants survived by swimming in a sea of broader civilian support, gained through either inspiring conviction or applying intimidation. They largely fought a classic counterinsurgency (COIN) campaign, focusing on constant, low-level attacks that chipped away at the enemy's resolve and manpower. Indeed, the VC's participation in the massive conventional Tet Offensive of 1968 proved virtually the organization's undoing; the VC losses were so high that it never again quite recovered its operational strength again.

The PAVN, by contrast, was a conventional army in every sense, with a manpower maintained at about 450,000 and operating Soviet- or Chinese-acquired armor and artillery, albeit in limited numbers compared to the Americans. The PAVN could and did fight a COIN war, infiltrating units into the South Vietnamese jungle hinterlands, but it also made several major offensive drives in an attempt to bring the war to an end—the Tet Offensive of 1968, the Easter Offensive of 1972, and the final victorious 1975 Spring Offensive. Its rolling war effort was fueled logistically by streams of porters shifting supplies from the North into the South via the Ho Chi Minh Trail through neighboring Laos and Cambodia.

Both the PAVN soldier and the VC insurgent were extremely poorly equipped compared to the American and indeed Army of the Republic of Vietnam (ARVN) forces, and they could rarely hope to gain fire superiority in any engagement that went on for more than a day or so. But despite the horrifying levels of battle casualties they suffered, they always returned with bloody persistence.

The following illuminating extract comes from *A Profile of the PAVN Soldier in South Vietnam* (1966), prepared for the Office of the Assistant Secretary of Defense/International Security Affairs and the Advanced Research Projects Agency by the influential RAND research and analysis institution. It is based upon interviews conducted with 40 PAVN defectors and POWs, and the purpose of the final report was "to portray the typical North Vietnamese soldier before he finds himself in Southern hands." Such information provided an insight into exactly who the U.S. infantryman was facing.

From *A profile of the PAVN Soldier in South Vietnam* (1966)

SUMMARY

This Memorandum is based on extensive interviews that a RAND team conducted with forty defectors and prisoners of war from North Vietnamese units fighting in South Vietnam. The purpose of the analysis is to portray the typical North Vietnamese soldier before he finds himself in Southern hands.

The portrait that emerges is of a man whom his government has sent to the South to fight, either as a quasi-volunteer or as a soldier following orders and told of his destination only after he was well on his way. By and large he is a man who has lived in considerable harmony with the Communist society from which he came. He seems thoroughly convinced that South Vietnam has been invaded by the Americans and needs his help to attain the fruits of victory for which the country struggled in the 1945–1954 war against the French. There is usually little doubt in his mind that the bombing of his homeland in the North is unjustified and evil.

The PAVN soldier, after the considerable ordeal of infiltrating the South via the Ho Chi Minh trail, encounters there some harsh realities. Though told by his cadres that the South is already overwhelmingly controlled by the VC, he is likely to find on arriving that he is not welcomed by the local people and must camp out in the jungle. Often he is taken aback to discover that he must fight his fellow Vietnamese. Or if this is not a surprise, that he must fight them in numbers greater than he has been led to expect. In addition to these unexpected setbacks, he learns that his training is not entirely suited to the type of war he must wage. As a result, his certainty of an early victory – though not necessarily his faith in the rightness of his cause – is sometimes shaken. In this process of disillusionment, he has been influenced only to a minor extent by propaganda emanating from the South. It is perhaps rather the prospect of a protracted war without victory that dispirits him most.

Despite manifold hardships and his wavering confidence in the outcome of the struggle, the North Vietnamese soldier, except in the still relatively rare instance when he defects, continues to fight tenaciously against the combined South Vietnamese–United States forces, partly because his faith in what he calls his mission remains unimpaired, and partly because his leaders employ physical and psychological devices to control his every thought and action. Among these devices are the three-man cell and the sessions of self-criticism. Both tend to keep him in line, though the latter often exasperate and even push him to, if not sometimes over, the brink of desertion.

The soldier depicted in the interviews appears to be an articulate young man of innate intelligence. Being skeptical, he is not easily won over to a sectarian point of view. For this reason, too, he is not ordinarily a doctrinaire Communist; he tends to accept some but not all of the Communist gospel. He is a man of resilience and endurance, able to bear hardships and other hazards to his morale, among which is notably his great distress at being separated from his family.

The study suggests that the PAVN soldier might be intensely vulnerable to a range of psywar appeals if these were well-designed, well-implemented, and well-orchestrated. Among the most profitable are likely to be those appeals that make it clear to him (1) that the war is unnecessary because what he believes to be the intention of the United States is simply a fiction created by his leaders; and (2) that his confidence in his ability to defeat the Americans as he did the French a decade earlier is grossly unrealistic.

[...]

BATTLE EXPERIENCE

Much of the PAVN's battle experience in the South is markedly undramatic or at least sounds that way in the interrogation report: "I was transferred upon my arrival in the South to a mortar and support unit in the 95th regiment. I took part in two engagements along National Route 19 in Gia Rai province. During these two engagements my unit gave support to other Front units. During all the time I was in the Front, the mission of my company was to support the other battalions in the division. That's all." Or, just as undramatically: "The cadre told us ... try to catch up with our battalion to participate in (an) attack.... On the way I felt sick and told the man in charge to walk ahead.... I got lost, and wandered for two days. I got scared and called the name of the man in charge of my group.... I heard a burst of gunfire. I lay down on the ground and after some time two American soldiers came and captured me." Or: "In October 1965 I ... received the order to attack Plei Me.... I fell seriously ill ... the medical personnel took me to a dispensary.... At about 8 or 9 AM helicopters landed American troops and we were all captured." Or, very similarly: "Finally (after 24 days in a bivouac area) my company received orders to go on an undisclosed operation.... After three days of marching I became so weak that I received orders to stay behind in the jungle with other sick men.... Finally the Americans landed in big helicopters near our hideout and captured all three of us."

Or, once again: "I was on a rice supply mission for my company, which was fighting at Plei Mei. When my team reached a clearing, we saw helicopters fly overhead, but we kept on walking. We were detected and strafed.... We ran in all directions. I don't know where the other fighters ran.... I stayed in the area. In the morning of the third day I was captured by the Americans."

The PAVN soldier might also be captured in a manner almost indistinguishable from surrender: "Our unit moved to set up an ambush for GVN parachutists ... we were to attack them if they arrived ... the Company Leader cautioned us to be very careful or we would be attacked by artillery from Plei Mei, which was about 10 to 12 miles from the ambush area. We stayed for three or four days waiting for the GVN soldiers. When they didn't appear, the men in my unit began to pack up and return to their former camp. A few of us (including myself) had been sick and were told to stay behind and rejoin our unit whenever we could. I heard a broadcast from a helicopter ... urging the Front fighters to put down their arms and surrender to the Nationalist Government. I thought to myself that if I stayed where I was I would surely die for lack of medicine.... If I surrendered to the Nationalists I might be able to stay alive ... I left my hiding place and went to where the Americans were. They captured me."

If our PAVN soldier is a non-commissioned officer, his account of his battle experience and capture might sound a little more martial: "After arriving in the South I participated in only one engagement.... On December 24 I went on an operation with my unit.... It was composed of 110 men. The soldiers were Northerners and the cadres were Northerners and regroupees.... The troops were enthusiastic and full or ardor.... They had participated only in a few engagements and never talked about fighting.... The operation took place on January 7, 1965.... We were not told about it at all beforehand.... At 3:00 AM the fighting started.... When I was ordered to fight I just fought without asking questions.... At 3:00 PM a GVN squad clashed with one squad of guerrillas.... Fifteen minutes later M-113s, coming from Hue, attacked us ... we were ordered to withdraw ... about 15 minutes later aircraft came to bomb our position.... I ran to the mountains and, upon returning to the village, was captured."

With regard to what he fears most, the PAVN's replies are contradictory. One type of airplane may inspire more fright in one PAVN than in another. The same is true for various kinds of ground attacks. No clear picture emerges as to what type of military action is considered most hazardous by the PAVN. But he does readily admit to being afraid of some weapons. He may also – atypically – claim not to be frightened at all: "When the fighting begins I'm so excited that I don't think of anything and therefore I'm afraid of nothing." Or perhaps of everything? It is hard to tell. The interviewers, trying to extract information on just exactly how the soldiers responded in actual operations, often drew inconclusive replies. The PAVN who will on occasion say that he was scared, and then again that he was not, discloses little about himself: whether he fights hard or competently, whether he panics when green, whether he responds well to his officers in combat, and so on. He is, of course, depressed by defeats and the sight of his dead comrades, just as he rejoices in his victories. But what soldier doesn't? Just how he feels in his "moment of truth" does not emerge clearly from the data. In any event, some PAVN are apparently rather tough and resourceful fighters, particularly some on the non-commissioned officers who were promoted while serving in the South.

The Vietnam War era was one in which the U.S. military was profoundly focused upon the theory and tactics of what we today call counterinsurgency (COIN) warfare. The Cold War between East and West primarily expressed itself in three forms: the threat of a nuclear exchange; the possibility of a major conventional war with the Soviets in Northern and Western Europe; and global, ideologically driven, insurgency conflicts. The first two remained thankfully theoretical, but COIN conflicts plunged much of the developing world into conflict at varying degrees of intensity.

The U.S. Army quickly realized that its infantry and all other branches needed doctrinal and tactical guidance on this aspect of warfare, especially as the United States became inexorably drawn into the Vietnam conflict. The Army's *Operations against Irregular Forces* (FM 31-15) came out in 1953, with revised versions in 1954 and 1961. The manual below, *Counterguerrilla Operations* (FM 31-16), was released in 1963. Although it was written to apply to all insurgencies, acknowledgement of what was happening in Vietnam was sewn into its fabric. At the time, the manual gave U.S. soldiers the best available insight into what they might have to face in terms of enemy forces in Vietnam, and how they might adapt their tactics accordingly.

From FM 31-16, *Counterguerrilla Operations* (1963)

CHAPTER 2
THE ENEMY RESISTANCE MOVEMENT

Section I. ORGANIZATION OF THE RESISTANCE MOVEMENT

3. General

a. A guerrilla force is the armed manifestation of a resistance movement by a portion of the population of the area against the local government or occupying power.

b. The fundamental cause of a resistance movement is the real, imagined, or incited dissatisfaction of a portion of the population with prevailing political, social, or economic conditions. Normally, this dissatisfaction will crystallize early in the resistance movement into a firm ideological base. This ideological base may be essentially positive in nature with such goals as national independence, economic and social improvements, or the securing of individual rights. However, many times, particularly during the early stages of a resistance movement, this base will be primarily negative with such goals as relief from actual or alleged oppression, elimination of foreign occupation, or elimination of exploitation and corruption.

4. Beginning of Resistance

a. Resistance movements begin when —

(1) Sufficient numbers of the population of an area become discontented with existing conditions which cannot be changed by peaceful and legal means, and

(2) A strongly motivated leadership element rises to lead the discontented population in its cause of changing the existing situation.

b. The movement focuses its initial attention on the spreading of the attitudes and beliefs of the early members of the movement to greater portions of the population, thereby turning discontent into disaffection and a willingness to participate in resistance activities.

c. Small groups then begin to live and work within the dissident order and gradually organize into underground elements that conduct covert activities to support the resistance movement.

d. The factors which inspire a resistance movement may arise internally in an area or country, or they may be created or assisted by "out-of-country" elements which desire to sponsor the movement for their own cause. Often, another country will lend support to a local resistance movement and attempt to control the movement to further its own aims.

5. Organization of a Resistance Movement

a. As elements of the population begin to group together for covert underground operations, the organization of the resistance movement is born. Thereafter, as the size of the movement grows, the organization develops along clearer and clearer lines. The organization of a resistance force differs from a regular force in that it is developed for a specific purpose, for specific terrain, and to combat a specific enemy. As the purpose, terrain, and enemy differ, the organization will vary.

b. Depending on the phase of growth the resistance movement has reached, it will vary in size from a few small groups to a large, complex, paramilitary organization of thousands of personnel. Once sufficient strength and civilian support is present, the small underground elements found in the early stages of the resistance movement will normally expand into an irregular force with two organized elements: an overt or guerrilla element, and a supporting covert or underground element. Both these elements depend on civilian and/or sponsoring power support to sustain themselves during operations. This civilian support is often called the "auxiliary." While one individual may operate both as a member of a guerrilla band and of a supporting underground cell of the irregular force, these two elements are discussed separately in the paragraphs below.

6. Guerrilla Force

a. The overt guerrilla arm of the resistance movement may vary from small groups to large paramilitary units of division or larger size with extensive support organizations. Large organizations normally include elements for combat, intelligence and counterintelligence, population control, and logistic support.

b. Members of large guerrilla units are usually severed from their normal civilian pursuits, while members of small guerrilla bands may alternately be either guerrilla fighters or apparently peaceful civilians. Members of guerrilla units may include —

(1) Civilian volunteers and persons impressed by coercion.

(2) Military leaders and specialists.

(3) Deserters.

(4) In active war, military individuals or small groups which have been cut off, deliberate stay-behind forces, escaped prisoners of war, and downed airmen.

c. In the advanced stages, guerrilla forces may consist of a regular army, regional troops, and the popular forces. The distinctions between these forces are based on differences in training, equipment, and mission.

(1) The regular army is the elite battle force and is normally not employed when there is a chance it may be defeated. The regular army is kept free to engage in a war of movement and to select the time and place for combat. It possesses the best equipment, weapons, and uniforms, has the highest pay, and is used strictly in its primary mission of defeating the conventional force opposing it. The regular army is organized along conventional lines and is well trained and led. It operates in close conjunction with the regional and popular forces. Fillers are usually selected from the best of the regional troops.

(2) The regional troops are less well organized, trained, and equipped than the regular forces. In the advanced stages, they are generally organized into battalions and regiments, and constitute the "mature guerrillas" in the true sense. One of the primary duties of the regional force is to protect the regular army while it is training and preparing for future operations. This force launches small attacks, harasses the enemy, keeps the enemy off balance, and ambushes reinforcements. Fillers are obtained from the popular troops.

(3) The popular troops are divided into two groups, a labor force and a home guard. The labor force is mainly responsible for collecting intelligence, making road repairs, building bases, fortifying villages, and acting as porters for the regular army. The members of the home guard receive limited military training and extensive political indoctrination. The home guard furnishes limited security for officials at village level.

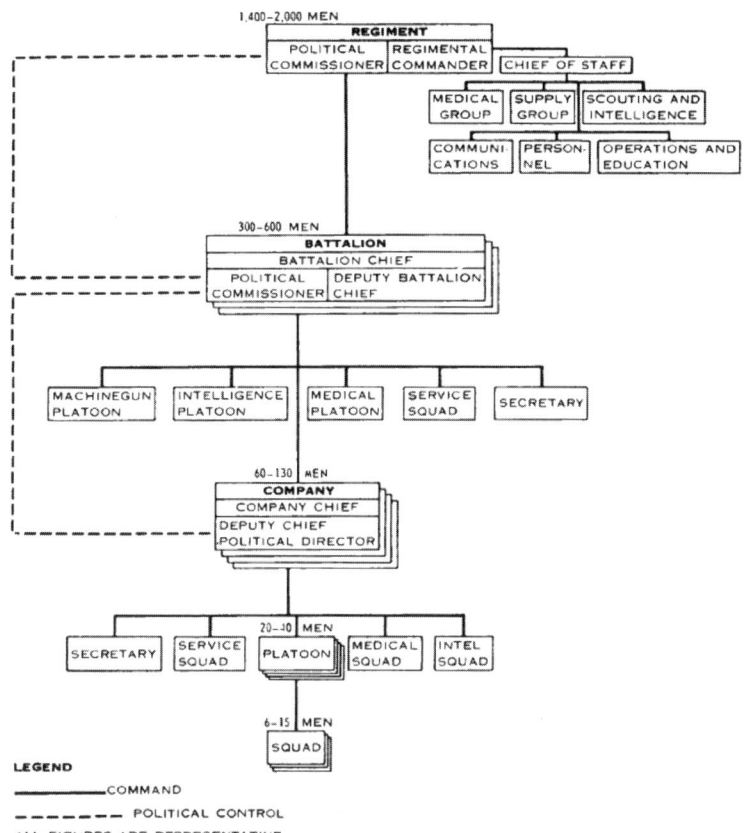

Typical guerrilla force organization.

7. The Underground

a. The underground element of a resistance movement must conduct most of its supporting activities in a covert manner because of the countermeasures used against it. Consequently, members of the underground usually maintain their identity as part of the civilian population. Successful underground organizations are compartmented by cells for security reasons. The cellular organization prevents one member, upon capture, from compromising the entire organization.

b. Covert resistance activities normally conducted by the underground may include espionage, sabotage, dissemination of propaganda and rumors, delaying or misdirecting orders, issuing false or misleading orders or reports of assassination, extortion, blackmail, theft, counterfeiting, and identifying individuals for terroristic attack.

c. The terroristic element of a resistance movement is normally a part of the underground organization. While terrorism will not normally be used extensively unless necessary, the maintenance of support for the resistance movement will normally dictate its employment.

d. Terrorism is the prime means of the resistance movement for the intimidation of the civilian population. It is used both to coerce individuals to actively support the movement and to force individuals to cease active resistance to it.

e. Since the methods used by the terroristic element normally do not conform to the professed moral base of the resistance movement, every means is used to indicate that the element arises from the civilian support for the movement rather than from the organized elements of the force. The terroristic element operates in an intensively covert and divorced fashion. Often, only a few members of the resistance movement will know who constitutes the terroristic element and the nature of its operations.

8. Civilian Support

a. In any civilian population there are certain individuals who are sympathetic to a resistance movement; but who, for various reasons, do not actively participate as members of the guerrilla force or underground. It is on these individuals the movement depends for the majority of its support.

b. It is often erroneously believed that the civil population of an area in which a resistance movement is active can be broken down into two general categories, those friendly to the resistance movement and those friendly to the local government or occupying power. Often, in fact, a great part of the population has no concern about the struggle and is sympathetic to neither combatant. Extreme care must be used in dealing with the civilian population in an effort to cultivate their support.

c. Since this neutral majority of the population is a prime target for counterguerrilla propaganda, the resistance movement will often use terroristic measures to insure that it does not become aligned with the forces countering the resistance movement.

9. Command

a. Successful guerrilla campaigns have invariably been characterized by intelligent leadership. Guerrilla forces that develop with little or no advance preparation are led by recognized local leaders who may or may not have a military background. When a recognized major guerrilla force leader lacks a military background, an allied sponsoring power may infiltrate qualified personnel to serve as military and technical advisors to the guerrilla commander. By so doing, the military capabilities of the guerrilla force are effectively exploited without destroying the command structure of the established organization.

b. Guerrilla forces organized as the result of extensive advance planning and preparation are normally commanded by personnel with an adequate military background.

10. Discipline

a. Far too often, the term "guerrilla" suggests a body of individuals entirely without discipline. Nothing could be more untrue. While spontaneously formed units may have poor discipline initially, it is not long before they learn that only with the strongest discipline can they succeed.

b. Effective guerrilla forces maintain strict discipline in all essential matters. It will surpass the discipline found in regular forces. It is enforced with quick and severe action, possibly without recourse to formal investigations and trials. Serious infractions or neglect of duty are often punished by death. To achieve surprise in operations, and security of the force, the guerrilla force commander has no alternative but to insist on implicit obedience to orders.

[…]

13. Supply

a. The continued existence of a guerrilla force and the extent to which it may be employed strategically or tactically depend on adequate supplies and equipment. In general, a guerrilla force lives off the land. The availability of food may often limit the size of the force that can be concentrated and the staying power of the force.

b. Food is normally procured from the populace by systematic levy. These levies are supplemented by raids on enemy supply depots and convoys. Other supply requirements including clothing, medical supplies, fuel, and communications equipment are procured locally. Arms, ammunition, demolitions, and other purely military-type materiel come from local caches, battlefield salvage, raids on enemy installations, and/or external sources. Guerrilla Forces may operate small factories to produce and repair military-type materiel.

c. As a general rule, the full potential of a guerrilla force in the latter and sophisticated stages of development can be exploited only if adequate supplies are infiltrated in from external sources. The amount of external logistic support may vary from small, irregular shipments of critical supplies to total support.

14. Evacuation and Hospitalization

a. Medical support in guerrilla warfare is often nearly nonexistent. Lack of evacuation facilities, hospitals, medical supplies, and trained personnel may preclude the organization of adequate medical support. A guerrilla force often uses existing civilian facilities to care for its sick and wounded, in which case the patients pose as civilians while undergoing treatment.

b. Historically, some guerrilla forces have been known to develop highly organized and effective medical support units and installations. Their organizations have paralleled those of regular forces and have included field hospitals located in inaccessible areas. They have recruited doctors, nurses, and technical personnel from the civilian population, and have obtained medical supplies from the local populace, from raids, and from external sources.

c. Guerrilla forces normally do not need the same degree of medical support or the extensive medical support backup required by regular forces. Most guerrilla operations are planned to result in comparatively few casualties. Employing surprise and basing its operations on excellent intelligence, the guerrilla force strikes weakly defended objectives or enemy forces unprepared to offer resistance. However, this advantage is offset to some degree by the increased requirement for medical care for sickness and infections resulting from continuous exposure to the elements and an inadequate diet.

15. Transportation

a. Guerrilla forces will utilize every means of transportation available. They develop a cross-country mobility difficult for a regular force to equal. The extent and kind of transportation used by a guerrilla force is limited by the area the force controls, the means at its disposal, and the topography. Historically, guerrillas have made extensive use of animals for mounts, pack animals, animal-drawn vehicles, and boats.

b. Forces that reach a high degree of development and that control large areas may be expected to use motor and mechanized ground vehicles and aircraft.

16. Communication

a. Communication is as important to guerrilla forces as to regular forces. Unified guerrilla forces establish efficient communication systems to exercise command, control, and coordination and to permit the flow of information. Intelligence, counterintelligence, security, and propaganda also depend upon communications. The nature of guerrilla force organization and operations makes radio the most flexible and effective way to fulfill the complex communications requirements.

b. Modern, portable, long-range radio transmitter-receiver equipment provides excellent communications for guerrilla forces. Other conventional and improvised communication means are used extensively. These include wire, visual means, and messenger service. Depending on the terrain, the existing situation, and the facilities available, the guerrilla force may use both mounted and foot messengers. Land communication nets over enemy-held territory are cleverly organized and operated. Women and children are often used as messengers. Every conceivable ruse will be used to conceal documents on messengers and to pass along information.

Section II. GUERRILLA FORCE OPERATIONS

18. Prerequisites for Successful Guerrilla Operations

a. Irrespective of whether a guerrilla force is operating in resistance to an established government or against an occupying power, the following are the minimum prerequisites for the successful operation of the force:

(1) *Civilian support.* Guerrilla forces must receive help from the civilians in the area. This help may be voluntary or may be forced through blackmail or terrorism. They furnish food, clothing, and other supplies, hideouts, transportation, and medical support to the guerrilla force. In addition, they act as home guards and provide integral parts of the guerrilla force intelligence and warning nets.

(2) *Outside assistance.* Often, assistance from an outside power will further bolster the support of the guerrilla force. A sponsoring power can assist in the routine supply and training of the guerrilla force and furnish adept leadership, funds, barter items, and complex items of military supply. Outside assistance, whatever its form, will usually give moral and psychological support to the resistance movement.

(3) *Favorable terrain.* Terrain gives advantage to a guerrilla force in direct proportion to the disadvantages it gives to the regular force combating it. Terrain such as jungles, mountain, swamps, etc., which restricts the observation, fire, communications, and mobility of the regular force is ideal for operations

of guerrilla forces. Until a guerrilla force has secured control of a large area, it must depend to a large degree on difficult terrain for the security of its base of operations.

(4) *Effective leadership.* See paragraph 9.

(5) *Unity of effort.* The responsibility for the development of strategy for a resistance movement must be extremely centralized; and once developed, must be rigidly adhered to by all elements of the force. The guerrilla force cannot tolerate strong internal rival factions. Within established strategy and policies, subordinate guerrilla commanders develop and execute their individual programs to exploit specialized situations and attack local targets of opportunity.

(6) *Discipline.* See paragraph 10.

(7) *Use of propaganda.* A guerrilla force must use propaganda to maintain confidence in its victory and sympathy in its cause among its civilian support.

(8) *Intelligence effort.* The survival of a guerrilla force depends on information about its enemy. It must continually operate extensive intelligence nets among the civilian population. Likewise, the guerrilla force cannot accomplish its operational missions without timely and accurate intelligence concerning its potential targets.

(9) *The will to resist.* Above all else, the guerrilla force must have a will to resist. From the devotion to the cause of the resistance movement comes the sustaining strength of the force. The cause may be national liberation, personal gain or aggrandizement, a political revolution, or the defense of some individual right. It may be a program of desperation against conditions so bad that all is to be gained and nothing lost by resistance. The single-minded devotion to a movement may cause the members of a guerrilla force to pursue an extremely fanatical course of action during the resistance movement.

19. Characteristics of Guerrilla Operations

a. A guerrilla force employs *surprise, mobility, and dispersion of forces* to demoralize the enemy and upset his current and projected operations. It normally seeks to paralyze the enemy force. Only in its latter stages of development, when it has achieved the semblance of a conventional force, will it attempt to destroy the enemy in actual combat. Guerrilla operations follow the same principles and methods of combat as conventional operations; only their application differs.

b. Surprise is a major requirement of success in guerrilla operations. To offset the enemy's superiority of forces and equipment, guerrillas strike where the enemy is weak and where he least expects an attack. Reliable intelligence and sound security enhance the surprise. Operations are conducted extensively in the hours of darkness and during periods of adverse weather conditions.

c. Mobility is another necessary requirement for the success of a guerrilla operation. Only when the guerrilla force has developed to the point where it can conduct conventional operations, will it attempt to match or surpass the ground vehicular or aerial mobility of its enemy. Quite conversely, in the earlier stages of development it will gain its mobility differential by operating in terrain which cannot be easily traversed by the mechanical mobility of the enemy. Mobility for the guerrilla force

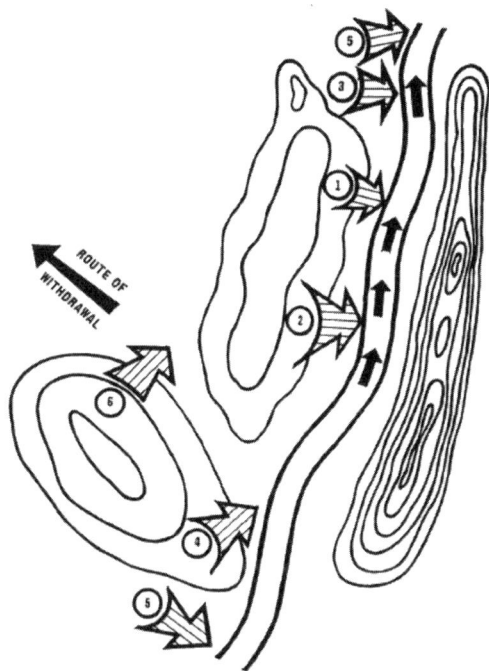

(1) ELEMENT TO HALT LEADING VEHICLE OR PARTY
(2) ASSAULT ELEMENTS
(3) ELEMENT TO ISOLATE ADVANCE GUARD
(4) ELEMENT TO CUT OFF RETREAT
(5) ELEMENT TO PREVENT REINFORCEMENT
(6) ELEMENT TO COVER WITHDRAWAL

Guerrilla-type ambush tactics.

comes from the extensive movement of small forces over a large area under the cloak of secrecy. A guerrilla band may strike and be miles away from the scene of the action before enemy reinforcements arrive.

d. Dispersion of forces is a principal characteristic of guerrilla operations. Normally, guerrilla operations are small-scale operations carried out over an extensive area. Guerrilla warfare is a war of detachment rather than mass contact; a war of quick paralyzing blows followed by swift withdrawals. Generally, guerrillas avoid pitched battles and seldom defend objectives. If hard pressed, they may disperse among the civilian population and then reassemble at a prearranged place.

"Tips on VC/NVA Booby Traps" was a short pamphlet issued to U.S. infantry and other ground troops in August 1967. It was absolutely timely, as each day, each week, the numbers of U.S. troops falling victim to VC booby traps crept ever higher. The ingenuity of the VC in designing and setting these remote killing and wounding devices was impressive as it was murderous. The most basic, but highly effective, was the punji pit, a simple hole in the ground, hidden with light foliage, with excrement-tipped wooden or bamboo spikes (sometimes iron nails driven through wood) at the bottom. The unsuspecting infantryman who stepped into such a trap would suffer penetrating lower limb injuries, with the excrement causing blood poisoning. One of the most famous victims of such a trap was the future Chairman of the Joint Chiefs of Staff, Colin Powell, when serving as a young infantry captain. Other booby traps included mines hidden behind or under logs; grenades, their pins already pulled, dragged out of tin cans by tripwire devices (this action released the grenade's priming lever, which had been restrained by the body of the can); swinging spiked balls of mud; and pre-tensioned bows and arrows, again tripwire operated. In total about 11 percent of U.S. Army deaths and 17 percent of injuries would be the result of booby traps.

From "Tips on VC/NVA Booby Traps" (August 1967)

Mines and booby traps can kill so be alert—stay alive.
If possible, don't be in too much of a hurry.
Never take anything for granted, it might look harmless but it might be a killer.
Evidence of old camouflage may indicate mines and booby traps.
Suspect all objects that appear loose or out of place.

Always look for trip wires.
Never bunch up and become a good target for command detonated mines. Destroy mines and booby traps in place or mark, report, and leave them alone.

Before cutting trip wires, check both ends for booby traps. Objects should not be disturbed without checking for booby traps. Only the enemy's imagination limits his use of mines and booby traps, remember that.
Be especially careful in areas where you are expected to slow down, bunch up or become a good target.
You can learn a lot from the local people, seek their help in locating mines and booby traps.

Trails and roads should be suspected. Check refilled holes, areas covered with straw or grass, littered with dung, pavement repairs, and other suspicious spots.
Report mines and booby traps immediately.
Always check your area for evidence of mines and booby traps when you set up your defense.

Probe gingerly when mines are suspected; don't depend solely on mine detectors. Since there was nothing in the area yesterday, don't assume there is nothing there today.

KNOWLEDGE INSPIRES CONFIDENCE.

REMEMBER

Mines and booby traps are favorite devices of the VC/NVA: grenades, spike traps, and AP and AT mines and a variety of other means are employed to harass, slow down, confuse and kill friendly forces. The forms of these weapons are limited only by the imagination of the designer.

Your best defense against mines and booby traps is

ALERTNESS
&
CAUTION

U.S. soldier carefully lifts a Viet Cong mine with his bayonet.

What a Platoon Leader Should Know About The Enemy's Jungle Tactics was released by the U.S. Army on October 12, 1967, by which time the U.S. Army infantry forces had acquired more than two years of frontline combat experience against the VC and PAVN. It was produced by the Combined Intelligence Center Vietnam, and its introduction was clear about its purpose: "The purpose of this handbook is to describe the jungle tactics, techniques, and deceptions which have been used over and over again by the enemy, often with alarming success. It is hoped that knowledge of these oft-repeated tactics will help the small unit leader to make a more intelligent assessment of the enemy situation by better understanding what to expect from the enemy during both movement and meeting engagements in the jungle." The picture painted by the handbook was of an intelligent and active foe, one that could never be patronized or underestimated without serious consequences. It was up to the platoon leaders to take this advice and turn it into sound tactical awareness, but their own experience would doubtless continue to add to the body of knowledge.

From *What a Platoon Leader Should Know About The Enemy's Jungle Tactics* (1967)

I. INTRODUCTION.

[…]

B. The terrain of South Vietnam ranges from rugged mountain peaks, 2500 meters high, to marshy plains below sea level. Much of this terrain is covered with dense rain forests that have become the traditional refuge for VC forces. Two distinct types of jungle are found in South Vietnam: the multicanopied forest with dense undergrowth, prevalent in the mountainous regions; and the mangrove swamps, peculiar to the Delta and coastal areas.

1. In I, II, and III Corps Tactical Zones, typical jungle terrain consists of a multicanopied forest with dense undergrowth. Generally, the trees are 25 to 30 meters high. Trees are two to three meters apart, and the distance between the ground and first foliation is 5 to 10 meters. Tree diameters vary from 40 to 150 centimeters (16 to 57 inches). The undergrowth consists of mosses, ferns, vines, bushes, briars, and grasses from one to three meters high. The bushes are two to three meters high, and vines and briars wind around the trees, extending up to the tree canopy. As elevation increases, the density of undergrowth decreases. At elevations higher than 1200 meters, an undergrowth of moss and grass is most prevalent. Throughout South Vietnam are many scattered forests of bamboo which are virtually impossible to travel through without first cutting a trail.

2. In IV Corps Tactical Zone, the terrain is subject to coastal flooding. Mangrove tidal swamps are very prevalent. The mangrove tidal swamp is a very dense evergreen forest growing in coastal areas flooded by the daily tide. The height of the trees ranges from 2 to 18 meters, averaging about 5 meters. They normally have a double-layered canopy, with the younger trees forming the lower canopy. Throughout the entire mangrove forest area there are many vines which hang down from the trees and twine among them. The undergrowth commonly consists of marsh grass, reeds, rushes, and palm bushes, usually about two meters high.

3. Some of the fiercest encounters involving company and platoon-sized actions have occurred in jungle terrain. There are several reasons why these engagements have often been costly for friendly forces:

a. The fight, on average, becomes joined at ranges between 12 and 20 meters, which are too close to afford any real advantage to our crew-served weapons.

b. Marking smoke, for air and artillery support, cannot be used effectively where the top canopy of the jungle is 15 to 20 meters high or triple thickness.

c. Over-eagerness, often resulting from the periods of fruitless search, causes small unit leaders to assault enemy positions without stopping to analyze the situation and to use all available firepower in coordination with good schemes of maneuver.

d. Supporting fires, to avoid striking friendly positions, must allow too wide a margin of error to influence the action.

e. Mortars are of no use unless they can be based where overhead clearance is available.

f. The advance of reinforcements is often erratic, ponderous, and exhausting.

g. Air medical evacuation is often difficult.

C. VC/NVA jungle warfare calls for repeated use of ambushes, mines, and boobytraps. This handbook points out those tactics and techniques which have often been used by the enemy in the past. The examples and illustrations covered in the handbook are not an attempt to cover the gamut of enemy jungle tactics. This would be impractical, if not impossible, to attempt in a single publication. The handbook is only an attempt to provide some conclusions concerning enemy jungle tactics based on reports provided by those small unit leaders who have encountered them in past operations.

II.   OFFENSIVE TACTICS.

A.   General. The ambush has been the most frequently and successfully used enemy offensive tactic in jungle terrain. Jungle ambushes are normally established on natural routes of movement such as trails and streams. They are characteristically short, violent actions followed by a rapid withdrawal.

B.   When Ambushes Can Be Expected. Enemy ambushes have been conducted at all hours of the day and night, however, as would be expected, the majority of ambushes occur during daylight hours. Almost 1/3 of all enemy ambushes occur during the morning hours, at which time friendly troops are moving out from their base camps to conduct daily operations. Often they have set up ambushes behind friendly patrols after they have left their patrol base. There have been cases in which patrols retraced their routes and were caught in ambushes when patrol members were tired and security was lax.

C.   Planning Ambushes.

1.   The enemy uses great patience in studying friendly movement methods and techniques. He is quick to detect patterns of regularity in friendly activity.

2.   The dense jungle undergrowth found in some areas, combined with the dark shadow of the canopy, limits ground observation to five meters; some enemy ambushes have been initiated at just that distance. Excellent fire discipline, particularly in the case of NVA units, has resulted in friendly elements walking within point-blank range of enemy small arms. The enemy initiates the action as close as possible in order to reduce the fire superiority and air power of friendly forces.

D.   Ambush Indicators. Based on observation and experience of small unit leaders, the following list of indicators has been compiled to assist platoon leaders in determining the likelihood of ambush sites in their area of operations:

1.   Tied-down brush. It may be a firing lane for an ambush site.

2.   Villages with no people present. They may conceal ambushes, but it should be remembered that the presence of civilians in an area does not preclude the possibility of an ambush. The VC often make themselves appear as "innocent" civilians in order to deceive friendly commanders into thinking the area is free of VC.

3.   Large herds of cattle and well-tended crops in a sparely populated area.

4.   An unusual amount of activity in a specific area. Activities which should be noted are reports of unknown units in the area and sightings of VC reconnaissance elements.

5. A steady delivery of small arms fire from one position. While this may appear to be aimed at checking or delaying movement, it may actually be designed to encourage pursuit.

6. Sniper fire. The enemy will use snipers to draw friendly forces into ambush positions. The snipers will fire harassing rounds; and, upon pursuit by the friendly forces, they will fall back and draw the force into an ambush.

E. Ambush Tactics and Formations. The enemy has used varying tactics and formations when initiating offensive actions. A few examples will illustrate some of the more common tactics which the enemy has successfully employed against friendly forces in the jungle. It should be remembered, however, that these formations and techniques vary according to the terrain, mission, and enemy units involved.

1. Lure and Ambush. The "lure and ambush" is a commonly used enemy tactic. The basic principle is to draw the attention of friendly forces and lure them into prepared positions. Many variations of this tactic have been noted during movement in jungle terrain. In one instance, a friendly platoon was patrolling near War Zone C. Several hundred meters short of its turn-around point it entered a keyhole-shaped jungle clearing, about 150 meters from treeline to treeline. The patrol entered the clearing in a column formation. When the head of the column was two-thirds of the way across the clearing, the point man spotted three enemy soldiers with their backs turned. They stood 15 meters to the left front of the column and 10 meters short of the treeline. Without turning, they darted away toward the jungle, and the lead files of the patrol turned to pursue. The turning of the column spread it neatly in front of the killing zone of an ambush, which was deployed just inside the treeline.

1. Lure and Ambush.

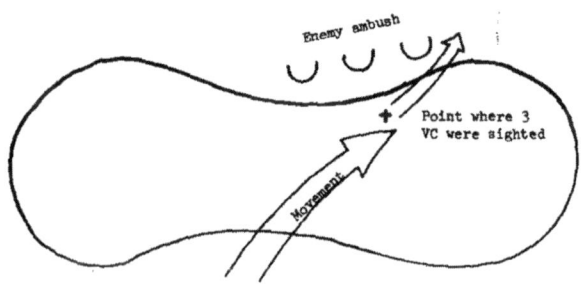

72

2. L-Shaped Ambush. In the L-shaped ambush, the long axis is normally positioned in a treeline and parallel to a road or trail. Deployment in an "L" formation enables the VC/NVA to mass a heavy concentration of fire both on the flank and down the length of a moving column. Employment of reserves adds flexibility to this type of ambush. Reserves can be used to reinforce either axis of the ambush, as a maneuvering element in enveloping friendly forces, and as a blocking force to cut off withdrawal routes or to ambush friendly reinforcements.

2. L-Shaped Ambush.

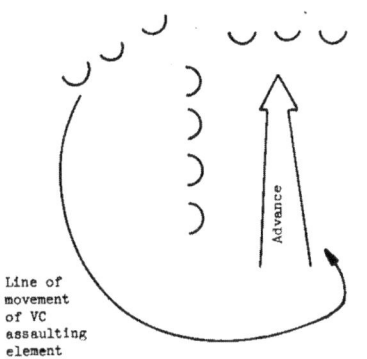

Line of movement of VC assaulting element

Advance

3. V-Shaped Ambush. The V-shaped ambush is usually positioned along a trail or path. Automatic weapons are placed at the vertex and down each side of the "V." This formation enables the enemy to place a heavy volume of fire on both flanks and down the length of an approaching column. Claymore mines have often been positioned in front of the automatic weapons to repel any attempt to roll up the flank or break through the ambush.

3. V-Shaped Ambush.

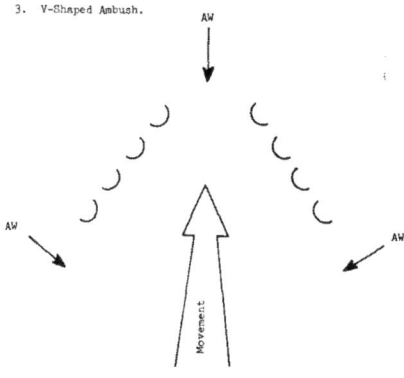

AW

AW

AW

Movement

4. U-Shaped Ambush. As with the L- and V-shaped ambushes, the "U" formation is also encountered during movement on jungle trails. The enemy places automatic weapons well to the front of the ambush site in order to seal off withdrawal from the trap. Claymores are also employed with this ambush formation.

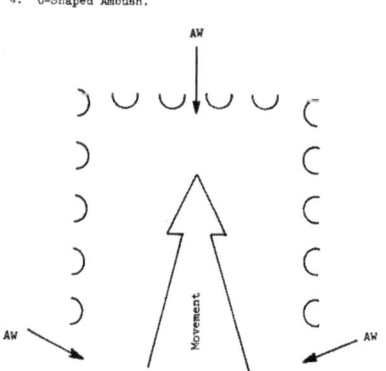

4. U-Shaped Ambush.

III. DEFENSIVE TACTICS.

A. General.

1. The enemy generally avoids the defense because he cannot withstand friendly firepower. However, he has tenaciously defended vulnerable units, bases, and installations for short periods of time. The enemy prepares extensive defensive positions throughout his operational areas. Defenses are prepared along trails and other avenues of approach. Boobytraps and mines are often incorporated into these defensive positions, particularly in base camp areas.

2. The enemy can move into an area and prepare bunkers and trench-lines overnight. If contacted, he attempts to hold these fortified positions throughout daylight hours, and then he withdraws in small groups over carefully planned escape routes during the hours of darkness. If cut off, he occupies one of many other fortified areas and resumes defensive tactics.

B. Characteristics of Field Fortifications. Increasingly, the enemy is employing extensive field fortifications in conjunction with his operations. VC/NVA soldiers are enthusiastic diggers because they fear friendly artillery and air strikes. These fortifications are characterized by:

1. Defense in depth.

2. Extensive use of camouflage.

3. Mutually supporting defensive networks.

4. Restricted avenues of approach.

5. Escape routes.

6. Use of boobytraps, mines, and obstacles.

7. Use of tunnels, bunkers, communication trenches, and foxholes.

C. Camouflage. Fortified areas almost always present the greatest difficulties to friendly forces. In no other technique is the enemy more skilled than in deceptive camouflaging of fortified base camps, supply caches, and villages. Nature is made to work in his favor; trees, shrubs, and earth are reshaped to conceal bunkers and trench lines. The density of the forest prevents observation from the air, and the thick undergrowth hinders ground forces from adequate observation of enemy base camps until after the camp has been discovered.

D. Fortified Enemy Base Camp. The fortified enemy base camp is roughly circular in form with an outer rim of bunkers and foxholes enclosing a complete system of living quarters. However, the shape will vary according to the terrain, the rise and fall of the ground, and the use of natural features to restrict attack on the camp to one or two avenues. Some of the enemy bases, particularly those used only for training or commo-liaison, have minimum defensive works. In all cases, the enemy is prepared to defend against a ground attack until forced to withdraw as a result of friendly pressure.

IV. WITHDRAWAL TACTICS.

A. General. The VC/NVA include a withdrawal plan for every offensive and defensive operation. They characteristically conduct rapid withdrawals along preplanned, concealed escape routes. The more common tactics for evasion, escape, and withdrawal include:

1. Fragmenting.

2. Dispersing.

3. Hiding.

4. Deceiving.

5. Delaying.

B. Types of Withdrawal. These examples of withdrawal tactics are typical of those encountered by small unit leaders throughout South Vietnam, particularly in jungle terrain.

1. Fragmenting. On one occasion an NVA regiment, discovered in an area removed from its normal base area, was overrun and larger amounts of supplies were captured and destroyed. As a result, all the subsequent contacts were with small groups of 3 to 10 men. The remnants of the regiment had fragmented to exfiltrate the battle area toward their base camp. Often when enemy battalions have been surrounded and forced to fight, their ammunition has been used up before the end of one day. These enemy units then split into small groups and attempt to break through the encirclement.

2. Dispersing. Another favorite technique used by small VC forces in danger of an unfavorable, close-range contact is to drop their packs and run. Friendly forces have been inclined to slow pursuit in order to inspect the packs.

3. Hiding. Hiding places available to the VC/NVA are innumerable, although underground locations appear to be the favorite. Underground hiding places for troops and equipment range from simple spider holes to elaborately reinforced rooms. From the surface these underground installations are extremely difficult to detect. Critical points are entrances and exits, which may be concealed in gardens, animal pens, river banks, under piles of straw or dung, and in or under structures. (See diagram of tunnel complex.)

4. Deceiving. VC/NVA forces have used deception to drawn friendly forces away from base camps. Small enemy units will harass and then withdraw in an attempt to swing the Allied direction of movement away from valuable areas.

5. Delaying. The VC/NVA have made extensive use of rear guard personnel to delay pursuing forces until withdrawal of the main element is accomplished. Also, ambushes designed to slow pursuers have often been employed.

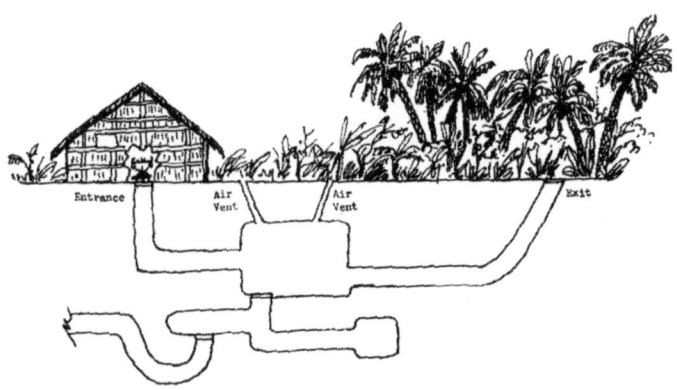

Extensive and ingeniously constructed underground tunnel systems are one of the unique features of the war in South Vietnam. They often fortified villages and base camps and have exits in concealed positions in the surrounding jungle.

MINES AND BOOBYTRAPS.

A. <u>Mines.</u> Enemy units do not make extensive use of conventional antipersonnel minefields in jungle terrain. Their present mine warfare doctrine calls for using numerous isolated mines and small groups of mines.

1. The VC/NVA rely heavily on the use of claymore mines. They employ both US and ChiCom claymores in all types of situations and engagements. Claymores are placed in trees, along trails, on perimeters of base camps and fortified villages, and at ambush sites.

2. One of the most common types of mines thus far encountered in jungle terrain is made with a ChiCom hand grenade. In enemy-controlled areas, these grenades are placed in well-travelled locations and detonated electrically. Thus, they can be controlled so that local people can walk back and forth over the area. When friendly troops are properly positioned, the enemy detonates the grenade. Long lead wires allow the person detonating the device to be well clear of the area. Grenades are sometimes buried in groups, producing the same effect as conventional antipersonnel mines.

B. <u>Boobytraps.</u> Ranging from a simple hole in the ground to a complicated device, the boobytrap is an effective way for then enemy to cause casualties and harass, delay, and confuse friendly forces at little cost to themselves. The variety of these weapons is limited only by the imagination of the designer. The same tricks the enemy uses to lure victims into ambush sites are used to lure them into boobytrapped areas.

1. Explosive boobytraps are employed in all phases of enemy operations from combat to sabotage. They are fired in the same manner as mines using the same types of firing devices and fuzes. Non-explosive boobytraps are frequently used in conjunction with mines at ambush sites. The enemy employs crude, but effective trip wire devices along trails and paths, which release arrows, bamboo whips, and other swinging, barbed, and club-type objects. Muddy trails and heavy vegetation can provide all the camouflage necessary for spike traps and punji pits. The enemy is extremely good at disguising his traps. A favorite enemy tactic is to mine and boobytrap areas which friendly elements have recently occupied. Upon returning to these areas, friendly personnel are often caught unaware by these new traps.

2. In conducting past searches of VC villages, base camps, and supply caches, boobytraps have often been located in the following places:

      a. In or near gates or entrances.

      b. Anywhere normal work does not take place (next to trails, in graveyards, near shrines, etc.).

      c. At entrances to concealed tunnels.

      d. In rubbish.

    e. On propaganda boards and flags displayed in conspicuous locations.

    f. Near animal pens or other enclosures.

    g. Under dung piles and dead foliage.

    h. Near wells.

3. The enemy has also rigged weapons, uniforms, dead bodies, binoculars, and many other objects with explosive boobytraps.

C. <u>Enemy Marking of Danger Areas.</u> VC/NVA units have found it necessary to follow certain procedures in marking mined and boobytrapped areas. As yet, no standard pattern for marking these areas appears to exist; different enemy units seem to have their own techniques for marking danger areas. The only apparent doctrine on marking mines and boobytraps is that a VC or NVA unit must know the location of mines and boobytraps within its own operational area. Also, it must coordinate with local forces for guidance on mine and boobytrap locations when operating in unfamiliar areas.

D. <u>Examples of Mine and Boobytrap Marking.</u> The following are examples of marking of mines and boobytraps which have been discovered by friendly elements. It should be remembered that all markers are subject to being disoriented by the effects of rain, wind, and animal and human movement through an area. Small unit leaders should insure that their personnel are thoroughly familiar with mine and boobytrap markings. Those presented in the illustrations should be anticipated at all times during movement along trails through jungle terrain. Many more types of markers are suspected to exist, and all personnel should be encouraged to report any new mine and boobytrap markers or indicators which are discovered. Doing this will aid in the reduction of friendly mine and boobytrap casualties.

1. Sign Markers

VUNG CÂM ĐỊA	TỬ ĐỊA	XIN ĐỪNG ĐI
Restricted Area Keep Away	Kill Zone	Please Don't Go

VUNG CÓ BẪY	VUNG CÓ GÀI BẪY
Area is Boobytrapped	Boobytrapped Area or Zone

Various handwritten signs have been encountered warning all persons entering an area that a danger exists if they pass the sign. The danger area is usually 50 to 200 meters beyond the signs. These signs are normally placed in enemy rear areas and are scheduled for removal in the event friendly troops conduct operations in the area.

    2. Parallel Sticks Marker.

Short sticks or lengths of bamboo laid parallel to a trail reportedly means that the trail is free of mines or boobytraps in I CTZ.

    3. Rock Markers on Trails.

Various formations of small rocks have been reportedly placed on trails to serve as a warning of mines and boobytraps ahead. These rock formations have been placed in circular, pyramid, and straight line patterns.

    4. Broken Bush Marker.

The VC break the top from a small sapling and strip most of the branches from it. One branch is left on the sapling and it points down the trail. Usually a mine or boobytrap has been found 50 to 100 meters down the trail.

    5. Grass Marker.

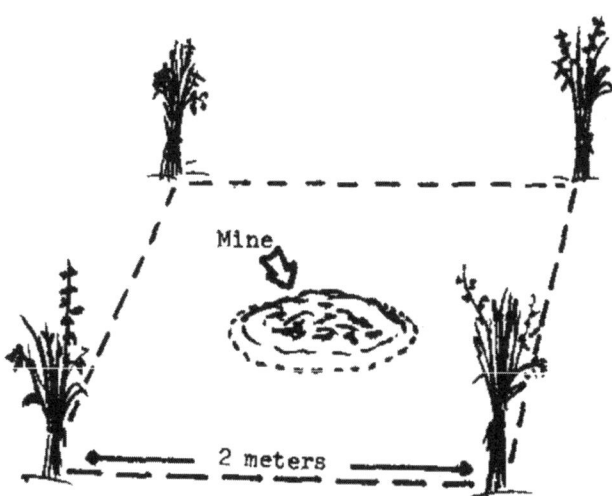

Growing grass is sometimes tied into four sheaves. The sheaves form a square with sides measuring approximately two meters. The mine is buried or concealed in the center of the square.

6. Red "X" Marker.

Red "X" signs are placed along trails leading to mined areas. This sign indicates a prohibited area and personnel should proceed with caution or by-pass the area. These signs have been found in both VC and GVN-controlled areas.

7. Broken Stick Marker.

A stick or length of bamboo broken at a right angle and lying across a trail has been used to warn of a mine or boobytrap 200 to 400 meters ahead.

8. Stakes and Leaves Marker.

These two warning signs have been reportedly used in the same area. One marker consists of two large leaves places parallel to each other on top of the mine or boobytrap. The second marker consists of two short sticks or stakes placed on the trail in front of and to the rear of the mine or boobytrap. These devices have been used individually and in conjunction with each other.

9. Bamboo Marker.

This marker consists of a small piece of bamboo six to eight inches long and a large joint of bamboo which is carved to fit over one end of the bamboo stick. The bamboo stick is stuck into the ground at about a 45° angle with the large end of the device pointing toward a mine or boobytrap.

10. Bamboo Tripod Marker.

The bamboo tripod marker consists of three pieces of bamboo approximately 18 inches long, tied together at one end and set up in a cone shape. Wire or another material is wrapped around the device near the bottom of the three legs so that the device will retain its cone shape. This device is placed over boobytraps, mines, and pungi pits.

VI. CONCLUSION.

A. VC/NVA jungle tactics call for repeated use of ambushes, mines, and boobytraps. They are used both separately and in combinations. The enemy is a master of camouflage and plans an ambush with great skill. He practices deception in all forms. He may lure you into a village or thick jungle by baiting you with a few men. When your initial estimate is light contact with a squad attempting to escape, the tendency is to pursue vigorously. Then, when the enemy has you positioned in the trap, he springs it. He holds his fire until you are well into the trap, and when he does spring it, he is almost on top of you.

B. Jungle warfare requires a reorientation from conventional tactics. A new approach to tactics and operations must be developed with greater emphasis on small unit tactics. Individual skills and tactics must be emphasized in order to allow small unit leaders to respond with the utmost flexibility to the perplexities and complications which are characteristic of jungle warfare. Getting to know the enemy better is the first step in solving the problem.

CHAPTER 4

INFANTRY TACTICS AND OPERATIONS

The ultimate objectives of U.S. infantry operations during the Vietnam War were generally brutally straightforward. During search-and-destroy missions, U.S. units were typically tasked with deploying around the last-known positions of enemy units, either through overland advance or airmobile landing, locating the enemy and his bases, and then destroying them. The success of the operation was measured by the body count and by the volume of enemy materiel seized or destroyed.

Tactically, these large operations were often characterized by movements designed to trap enemy forces either against the terrain or, more commonly, between multiple units at different locations. A classic action might be the "hammer and anvil," in which one force—the hammer—would advance directly against the enemy positions, driving the VC and NVA back until they met the anvil—another force in either static or mobile positions lying across the enemy's line of retreat. Alternatively, U.S. forces would wrap around the enemy with wide constricting arms, channeling him into a confined pocket of ground where he could be smashed by massive American support fire. Ideally, the operations were intended to throw a tight enough net that no enemy would escape, but the VC and NCA understanding of terrain and escape routes meant that this was rarely the case.

Yet aside from the major tactical operations, the ground war in Vietnam was also conducted in thousands of minor engagements, small in overall scale but brutal and intense at the point where they were fought. FM 31-14, *Operations Against Irregular Forces* (1961), acknowledged that "small-unit actions" were a defining characteristic of COIN warfare. The following extract explains the factors in operational planning, but also indicates something of the diversity of COIN missions. What is clear is the need to take and seize the initiative quickly, overcoming through speed and violence of action the enemy's advantages in terrain, dispersal, and movement.

From FM 31-15 *Operations Against Irregular Forces* (1961)

Section II. PLANNING

12. General

a. Operations against irregular forces are designed to establish control within the resistance area, eliminate the irregular force, and assist in the reconstruction, rehabilitation, and reeducation required to provide a suitable atmosphere for peaceful living. These goals are sought concurrently, but in specific instances priorities may be established. The specific actions required to attain each goal are often the same, and even when different, are usually planned and conducted concurrently.

b. Operations against irregular forces are planned according to these basic considerations.

(1) The majority of operations consist of small unit actions.

(2) Operations are primarily offensive in nature; once initiated, they are continued without halt to prevent irregular force reorganization and resupply. Lulls in irregular activities or failure to establish contact with hostile elements may reflect inadequate measures in the conduct of operations rather than complete success.

(3) Operations are designed to minimize the irregular force's strengths and to exploit their weaknesses.

(a) The greatest strength of an irregular force lies in its inner political structure and identification with a popular cause, its ability to conceal itself within the civil population, the strong motivation of its members, and their knowledge of the resistance area.

(b) The greatest weakness of an irregular force lies in its dependence upon support by the civil population; its lack of a reliable supply system for food, arms, and ammunition; and its lack of transportation, trained leadership, and communications.

(4) The close relationship between the civil population and the irregular force may demand enforcement of stringent control measures. In some cases it may be necessary to relocate entire villages, or to move individuals from outlying areas into population centers. It may be necessary to relocate those who cannot be protected from guerrilla attack, and those who are hostile and can evade control.

c. Terrain and the dispositions and tactics of guerrilla forces usually limit the effectiveness of artillery. However, the demoralizing effect of artillery fire on guerrillas often justifies its use even though there is little possibility of inflicting material damage. Ingenuity and a departure from conventional concepts often make artillery support possible under the most adverse circumstances.

d. The rough terrain normally occupied by guerrilla forces often limits the use of armored vehicles. However, armored vehicles provide protected communications, effective mobile roadblocks, and convoy escort. Planning should therefore include the employment of armor whenever its use is feasible. When used against guerrillas, armored vehicles must be closely supported by infantry, as guerrillas are skilled at improvising antitank means and may be equipped with recoilless weapons and light rockets.

e. The helicopter has wide application when used against irregular forces, subject to the usual limitations of weather and visibility. Its capability for delivering troops, supplies, and suppressive fires, and its ability to fly at low speed, to land in a small clearing, and to hover make it highly useful.

f. Morale of forces engaged in operations against irregular forces presents some planning considerations not encountered in other types of combat. Operations against a force that seldom offers a target, disintegrates before opposition, and then re-forms and strikes again where it is least expected may induce strong feelings of futility among soldiers and dilute their sense of purpose.

g. Activities between adjacent commands must be coordinated to insure unity of effort. If a command in one area carries out vigorous operations while a neighboring command is passive, guerrilla elements will move into the quiet area until danger has passed. Underground elements will either remain quiet or transfer their efforts temporarily.

h. Definite responsibilities for the entire area of operations are specified, using clearly defined boundaries to subdivide the area. Boundaries should not prevent hot pursuit of irregular force elements into an adjacent area. Coordination should, however, be accomplished between affected commands at the earliest practicable opportunity. Boundaries should be well defined and should not bisect swamps, dense forests, mountain ridges, or other key terrain features used by guerrilla elements for camps, headquarters, or bases. Similarly, well-defined boundaries should be used to divide urban areas to insure complete coverage.

i. Terrain and the dispositions and tactics of guerrilla forces furnish excellent opportunity for the employment of chemical and biological agents and riot control agents. Operations against irregular forces should evaluate the feasibility of chemical and biological operations to assist in mission accomplishment.

13. Planning Factors

a. Planning for operations against irregular forces requires a detailed analysis of the area concerned and its population. Close attention is given to both the civil (political, economic, social) and the military situations.

b. The following specific factors are considered in the commander's estimate:

(1) The motivation and loyalties of various segments of the population, identification of hostile and friendly elements, vulnerability of friendly or potentially friendly elements to coercion by terror tactics, and susceptibility to enemy and friendly propaganda. Particular attention is given to the following:

(a) Farmers and other rural dwellers.

(b) Criminal and tough elements.

(c) Adherents to the political philosophy of the irregular force or to similar philosophies.

(d) Former members of armed forces.

(e) Existence of strong personalities capable of organizing an irregular force and their activities.

(2) The existing policies and directives regarding legal status and treatment of civil population and irregular force members.

(3) The terrain and weather to include—

(a) The suitability of terrain and road and trail net for both irregular force and friendly force operations.

(b) The location of all possible hideout areas for guerrillas.

(c) The location of possible drop zones and fields suitable for the operation of aircraft used in support of guerrilla units.

(4) The resources available to the irregular force, including—

(a) The capability of the area to furnish food.

(b) The capability of friendly forces to control the harvest, storage, and distribution of food.

(c) The availability of water and fuels.

(d) The availability of arms, ammunition, demolition materials, and other supplies.

(5) Irregular force relations with any external sponsoring power, including—

(a) Direction and coordination of irregular activities.

(b) Communication with the irregular force.

(c) Capability to deliver organizers and supplies by air, sea, and land.

(6) The extent of irregular force activities and the force organization to include—

(a) Their origin and development.

(b) Their strength and morale.

(c) The personality of the leaders.

(d) Relations with the civil population.

(e) Effectiveness of organization and unity of command.

(f) Status of equipment and supplies.

(g) Status of training.

(h) Effectiveness of communications.

(i) Effectiveness of intelligence, including counterintelligence.

(7) The size and composition of forces available for counteroperations to include–

(a) Own forces.

(b) Other military units within the area.

(c) Civil police, paramilitary units, and self-defense units.

(8) The communication facilities available to allow effective control of forces engaged in counteroperations.

Section III. PROPAGANDA AND CIVIC ACTION

14. Propaganda

a. Propaganda is planned and employed in the campaign to achieve the following immediate goals:

(1) Divide, disorganize, and induce defection of irregular force members.

(2) Reduce or eliminate civilian support of guerrilla elements.

(3) Dissuade civilians from participating in covert activities on the side of the irregular force.

(4) Win the active support of noncommitted civilians.

(5) Preserve and strengthen the support of friendly civilians.

(6) Win popular approval of the local presence of friendly military forces.

(7) Obtain national unity or disunity as desired.

b. Propaganda activities aimed at achieving the immediate goals cited above must, as a minimum, be in consonance with each of the desired long-range goals, and should where possible contribute to their attainment.

c. For purposes of planning and directing the propaganda program, the population is divided into five target audiences. These are—

(1) Guerrilla units.

(2) Underground elements.

(3) Those civilians who provide information, supplies, refuge, and other assistance to the guerrillas and the underground.

(4) The noncommitted civil population.

(5) Friendly elements of the civil population.

d. Propaganda themes are based on the recognizable aspects of friendly economic and political programs and on potentially divisive characteristics of hostile target audiences. Possible divisive factors are—

(1) Political, social, economic, and ideological differences among elements of the irregular force.

(2) Rivalries between irregular force leaders.

(3) Danger of betrayal.

(4) Harsh living conditions of guerrilla elements.

(5) Scarcity of arms and supplies.

(6) Selfish motivation of opportunists and apparent supporters of the resistance movement.

[...]

15. Civic Action

a. Civic action is any action performed by the military force utilizing military manpower and material resources in cooperation with civil authorities, agencies, or groups, which is designed to secure the economic or social betterment of the civilian community. Civic action can be a major contributing factor to the development of favorable public opinion and in accomplishing the defeat of the irregular force. Military commanders are encouraged to participate in local civic action projects wherever such participation does not seriously detract from accomplishment of their primary mission.

b. Civic action can include assistance to the local population as construction or rehabilitation of transportation and communication means, schools, hospitals, and churches; assisting in agricultural improvement programs, crop planting, harvesting, or processing; and furnishing emergency food, clothing, and medical aid as in periods of natural disaster.

c. Civic action programs are often designed to employ the maximum number of civilians until suitable economy is established. The energies of civilians should be directed into constructive channels and toward ends which support the purpose of the campaign. Unemployed and discontented masses of people, lacking the bare necessities of life, are a constant hindrance and may preclude successful accomplishment of the mission.

d. Civic action is an instrument for fostering active civilian opposition to the irregular force and active participation in and support of operations. The processes for achieving an awareness in civilian populations of their obligation to support stated aims should begin early. Commanders should clearly indicate that civil assistance by the military unit is not simply a gift but is also action calculated to enhance the civilians' ability to support the government.

e. Civil affairs units of the TOE 41-series are employed to assist in the conduct of civic action projects and in the discharge of civil responsibilities.

[…]

Section V. COMBAT OPERATIONS

23. General

a. Combat operations are employed primarily against the guerrilla elements of an irregular force. However, underground elements sometimes attempt to incite large-scale organized riots to seize and hold areas in cities and large towns; combat operations are usually required to quell such uprisings.

b. Combat tactics used against guerrillas are designed to seize the initiative and to ultimately destroy the guerrilla force. Defensive measures alone result in an ever-increasing commitment and dissipation of forces and give the guerrillas an opportunity to unify, train, and develop communications and logistical support. A defensive attitude also permits the guerrillas to concentrate superior forces, inflict severe casualties, and lower morale. However, the deliberate use of a defensive attitude in a local area as a deceptive measure may prove effective.

c. Constant pressure is maintained against guerrilla elements by vigorous combat patrolling and continuing attack until they are eliminated. This keeps the guerrillas on the move, disrupts their security and organization, separates them from their sources of support, weakens them physically, destroys their morale, and denies them the opportunity to conduct operations. Once contact is made with a guerrilla unit, it is maintained until that guerrilla unit is destroyed.

d. Surprise is sought in all operations, but against well-organized guerrillas it is difficult to achieve. Surprise may be gained by attacking at night, or in bad weather, or in difficult terrain; by employing small units; by varying operations in important particulars; and by unorthodox or unusual operations. Counterintelligence measures are exercised throughout planning, preparation, and execution of operations to prevent the guerrillas from learning the nature and scope of plans in advance. Lower echelons, upon receiving orders, are careful not to alter their dispositions and daily habits too suddenly. Tactical cover and deception plans are exposed to guerrilla intelligence to deceive the guerrillas as to the purpose of necessary preparations and movements.

e. The military force attacks targets such as guerrilla groups, camps, lines of communication, and supply sources. Unlike normal combat operations, the capture of ground contributes little to the attainment of the objective since, upon departure of friendly forces, the guerrillas will reform in the same area. Specific objectives are sought that will force the guerrillas to concentrate defensively in unfavorable terrain, and that will facilitate the surrender, capture, or death of the maximum number of guerrillas.

Men of C Company, 16th Infantry, 1st Infantry Division, come under sniper fire during a search-and-destroy mission near Bien Hoa, October 4, 1965.

f. Those guerrilla elements willing to fight in open battle are isolated to prevent escape and immediately attacked. Guerrilla elements which avoid open battle are forced into areas which permit containment. Once fixed in place, they are attacked and destroyed. Consideration should be given to the employment of chemical agents to assist in these actions.

g. When the guerrilla area is too large to be cleared simultaneously, it is divided into subareas which are cleared individually in turn. This technique requires the sealing off of the subarea in which the main effort is concentrated to prevent escape of guerrilla groups. Once a subarea is cleared, the main combat force moves to the next subarea and repeats the process. Sufficient forces remain in the cleared area to prevent the development of new guerrilla groups and to prevent the infiltration of guerrillas from uncleared areas. Pending the concentration of a main effort in a subarea, sufficient forces are employed to gain and maintain contact with guerrilla units to harass them, and to conduct reaction operations.

24. Reaction Operations

a. Reaction operations are those operations conducted by mobile combat units, operating from static security posts and combat bases, for the purpose of reacting to local guerrilla activities. When a guerrilla unit is located, the reaction force deploys rapidly to engage the guerrilla unit, disrupt its cohesion, and destroy it by capturing or killing its members. If the guerrilla force cannot be contained and destroyed, contact is maintained, reinforcements are dispatched if needed, and the guerrillas are pursued. Flank elements seek to envelop and cut off the retreating guerrillas. The guerrillas should be prevented from reaching populated areas where they can lose their identity among the people, and from disbanding and disappearing by hiding and infiltration. When escape routes have been effectively blocked, the attack is continued to destroy the guerrilla force. The mobility required to envelop and block is provided by ground and air vehicles and by rapid foot movement.

b. Reaction operations are simple, preplanned, and rehearsed because the majority of actions will be required at night. To gain this end the area and possible targets for guerrilla attack must be known in detail. Common targets include desolate stretches and important junctions of roads and railroads, defiles, bridges, homes of important persons, military and police installations, government buildings, public utilities, public gathering places, and commercial establishments. Primary and alternate points are predesignated for the release of re-action forces from centralized control to facilitate movement against multiple targets. Such points are reconnoitered and are photographed for use in planning and in briefing. Within security limitations, actual release points are used during rehearsals to promote complete familiarity with the area.

25. Harassing Operations

a. Harassing operations prevent guerrillas from resting and regrouping, inflict casualties, and gain detailed knowledge of the terrain. They are executed by extended combat patrols and larger combat units. Specific harassing missions include— reconnaissance to locate guerrilla units and camps; raids against guerrilla camps, supply installations, patrols, and outposts; ambushes; marketing [*sic*] targets; assisting major combat forces sent to destroy guerrilla groups; and mining guerrilla routes of communication.

b. Harassing operations are conducted night and day. Operations at night are directed at guerrillas moving about on tactical and administrative missions. Operations during the day are directed at guerrillas in their encampments while resting, regrouping, or training.

26. Denial Operations

a. Operations to deny guerrilla elements contact with, and support by an external sponsoring power, are initiated simultaneously with other measures. Denial operations require effective measures to secure extensive border or seacoast areas and to preclude communications and supply operations between a sponsoring power and guerrilla units.

b. The method of contact and delivery of personnel, supplies, and equipment whether by air, water, or land must be determined at the earliest possible time. Border areas are secured by employing border control static security posts, reaction forces, ground and aerial observers, listening posts equipped with electronic devices, and patrols. When time and resources permit, wire and other obstacles, minefields, cleared areas, illumination, and extensive informant nets are established throughout the border area. Radio direction finding and jamming, and Navy or Air Force interdiction or blockade elements may be required.

27. Elimination Operations

a. Elimination operations are designed to destroy definitely located guerrilla forces. A force much larger than the guerrilla force is usually required. The subarea commander is normally designated as overall commander for the operation. The plan for the operation is carefully prepared, and the troops are thoroughly briefed and rehearsed. Approaches to the guerrilla area are carefully reconnoitered. Deception operations are conducted to prevent premature disclosure of the operation.

b. The encirclement of guerrilla forces is usually the most effective way to fix them in position so as to permit their complete destruction.

(1) If terrain or inadequate forces preclude the effective encirclement of the entire guerrilla held area, then the most important part of the area is encircled. The encirclement is made in depth with adequate reserves and supporting elements to meet possible guerrilla attack in force and to block all avenues of escape.

(2) The planning, preparation, and execution of the operation are aimed at sudden, complete encirclement that will totally surprise the guerrillas. The move into position and the encirclement is normally accomplished at night to permit maximum security and surprise. The encirclement should be completed by daybreak to permit good visibility for the remainder of the operation.

(3) Support and reserve units are committed as required to insure sufficient density and depth of troops and to establish and maintain contact between units. Speed is emphasized throughout the early phases of the advance to the line of encirclement. Upon arriving on the line of encirclement, units occupy defensive positions. The most critical period in the operation is the occupation of the line of encirclement, especially if the operation is at night. Large guerrilla formations may be expected to react violently upon discovering that they have been encircled. The guerrillas will probe for gaps and attack weak points to force a gap. Escape routes may be deliberately established as ambushes.

(4) Units organizing the line of encirclement deploy strong patrols to their front. Air reconnaissance is used to supplement ground reconnaissance. Reserves are committed if guerrilla forces succeed in breaking through or infiltrating the line of encirclement.

(5) Once the encirclement is firmly established, the elimination of the guerrilla force is conducted methodically and thoroughly. A carefully controlled contraction of the perimeter is begun, which may be conducted in any one of three ways:

(a) By a simultaneous, controlled contraction of the encirclement.

(b) By driving a wedge through the guerrilla force to divide the area, followed by the destruction of the guerrillas in each subarea.

(c) By establishing a holding force on one or more sides of the perimeter and tightening the others against them.

(6) During any of the foregoing maneuvers the units that advance from the initial line of encirclement must be impressed with the necessity of thoroughly combing every possible hiding place for guerrilla personnel and equipment. Successive echelons comb all the terrain again. Areas that appear totally inaccessible, such as swamps or marshes, must be thoroughly searched.

Guerrilla ruses discovered during the operation are reported promptly to all participating units and agencies. All local individuals, including men, women, and children, found in the area are held in custody and are released only after identification and on orders from appropriate authority.

c. Lack of time, inadequate forces, or the terrain may prevent encirclement operations. Surprise attacks followed by aggressive pursuit may prove successful in these cases. The position, probable escape routes, and strength of the guerrilla forces must be ascertained before launching the operation. Ambushes should be established early on possible escape routes. Patrolling should be conducted in a manner designed to confuse the guerrillas as to specific plans or intentions. Chances of achieving surprise are increased by using airmobile or airborne forces, and by inducing trustworthy local guides who are thoroughly familiar with the terrain and guerrilla disposition to collaborate and guide the attacking force over concealed routes.

d. After a successful attack on a guerrilla formation, the area is combed for concealed guerrilla personnel and equipment. Documents and records are collected for intelligence analysis. Ambushes are retained along trails in the area for extended periods to kill or capture escapees and stragglers from the guerrilla force.

28. Combat in Urban Areas

a. Underground elements in cities and towns often incite organized rioting, seize blockwide areas, erect street barricades, and resist any attempts to enter the area. Nonparticipants caught in the area are usually held as hostages. The objectives of these operations are to commit the countering force to actions against the civil population which will result in a gain of sympathizers for the irregular force and make it appear that the irregular force is promoting a popular cause.

b. When an urban area has been seized it must be reduced as soon as possible to prevent an apparent success or victory by the irregular force, to maintain popular support for the friendly cause, and to free troops for use elsewhere. The operations required to reduce it resemble normal street and house-to-house fighting. The following tactics are employed:

(1) A cordon is established to surround and seal the barricaded area. The cordon is established at the next street or road, out from the barricaded area, which offers good visibility, fields of fire, and ease of movement. All unauthorized personnel are cleared from the intervening area. The cordon controls all movements into and out of the encircled area.

(2) Announcement is made to the insurgents by such means as loudspeakers and leaflets, that the area will be attacked at a given time unless they lay down their arms, return their hostages safely, and surrender peacefully. Amnesty and protection may be offered to those who surrender prior to the attack.

(3) Maneuver and fire elements attack at the stated time and clear the area as rapidly as possible, with a minimum of killing and destruction of property. The cordon remains in place to maintain security, support the attack by fire where possible, and receive prisoners and rescued hostages from the attacking elements.

(4) If the area is large it is divided into sectors for control purposes. As each sector is cleared, the cordon moves in to exclude it; close surveillance of cleared areas is maintained in case underground passageways are used as escape routes. Succeeding sectors are attacked and cleared one at a time.

The following passages from FM 31-30, *Jungle Training and Operations* (1965), focus on two of the most critical infantry skillsets of the Vietnam War—effective patrolling and ambush/counterambush tactics. Tens of thousands of U.S. infantry spent endless hours on patrol, hunting for an elusive enemy in terrain that often reduced visibility to a few yards. The challenge for soldiers was to stay alert, focused, and disciplined at all stages of the patrol, even when days of heat and humidity dulled the senses and the powers of attention. The "point man" had the unenviable duty of leading the way at the front, scanning the terrain for signs of booby traps and ambushes. An infantryman who regularly took point might have had a life expectancy of four to six weeks. Another exposed individual was the radio operator, who lugged around a heavy piece of equipment whose bulk, antenna, and tactical importance made him a natural target for the enemy.

An uneventful patrol might suddenly explode in an enemy ambush, the primary U.S. infantry response being to go to ground and return fire in superior volumes, enabling the U.S. troops to regain some movement initiative. Sometimes, though, it would be the U.S. troops planning and launching the ambush, and here they could be inventive. An infantry veteran interviewed by the author (a former platoon leader) described how in planning an ambush he had his troops lay meters of detcord (explosive cable used for linking demolitions charges) just under the soil along an irrigation ditch by the side of a trail. When the Americans ambushed a VC unit on the trail, the VC soldiers all leapt for cover into the ditch, whereupon the detcord exploded, killing most of them. There was no room for mercy on either side.

From FM 31-30, *Jungle Training and Operations* (1965)

Section II. UNITS

39. General

a. General. Contacts with enemy forces in the jungle will usually be sudden, violently fought encounters between small troop elements. Primarily, such actions will be fought by patrols where the essential requirements for success will be strong and effective junior leadership and high state of training of the individual soldier. High standards can only be achieved and maintained by a progressive program from individual through unit training.

b. Training Priorities.

(1) *First priority.* Commanders should arrange training programs to require drill, practice, and rehearsals until proficiency of units is attained in the following subjects and skills:

(a) Patrolling.

(b) Ambush.

Soldiers of the 1st Cavalry Division (Airmobile) during Operation *White Wing*, February 19, 1966.

(c) Counterambush.

(d) Guerrilla and counterguerrilla operations.

(e) Jungle base operations.

(2) *Second priority.* The following subjects are important and may be readily combined with first priority training activities. Maximum integration of the following subjects should be effected during all unit jungle training:

(a) Small boat handling techniques (to include improvised obstacle crossing expedients).

(b) Communications and communications expedients.

(c) Supply and evacuation techniques.

(d) Construction of trails, bridges and roads.

(e) Identification and engagement of aircraft.

40. Patrolling

a. General. Patrolling is important in all types of warfare; however, it has increased importance under jungle conditions, especially against guerrilla forces. Patrol techniques for the jungle are not basically different, but because of the terrain, vegetation and usual guerrilla jungle tactics, some modifications to normal technique and methods are advisable. [...]

b. Types and Missions. Patrols are classified as either reconnaissance or combat, the designation generally indicating the mission.

(1) *Reconnaissance patrols.* These are small patrols which are sent out to seek information by stealth, avoiding contact with the enemy. A reconnaissance patrol in the jungle should not exceed 6 men due to the difficulty in moving silently through dense vegetation; a larger number of men is liable to cause noise which would increase chances of detection. Because of the usual scarcity of information about the terrain and the probable unfamiliarity of troops with the lay of the ground, these patrols should be detached from a combat patrol, if possible. The combat patrol will then have the advantage of some members who are familiar with the terrain in the immediate vicinity. This would be especially advantageous if the combat patrol is sent out over the same routes used by the reconnaissance element.

(2) *Combat patrol.* These patrols may vary in size from a squad to a company. Generally, a combat patrol is dispatched to contact and eliminate an enemy force or installation. In jungle operations this type of patrol may be assigned specific missions to—

(*a*) Attack enemy patrol bases.

(*b*) Attack guerrilla base camps and/or destroy their cultivations.

(*c*) Pursue a guerrilla force after attack by a larger unit or after a guerrilla raid or incident.

(*d*) Ambush enemy elements.

(*e*) Dominate or interdict an area to prevent guerrilla elements from contacting friendly civilian elements.

(*f*) Search (or "sweep") specified areas.

(3) *Common mission.* All patrols are a source of intelligence and must be prepared to report all information, topographical or enemy, which is discovered. Combat patrols are often a better source of information than a reconnaissance patrol because combat patrols contain more men who are able to observe, remember, and report enemy activities, terrain characteristics or other important and unusual occurrences. Further, a combat patrol usually is successful in finding and fighting the enemy. As a result, members are in a position to find more about the enemy, his equipment, his morale, his fighting qualities, and his state of training, than are members of a patrol whose mission is merely to observe the enemy without contacting him. The mission of intelligence cannot be overemphasized in the jungle because of

the difficulty in obtaining accurate information. In training, troops should be continually reminded that they represent the primary means to acquire such detailed information.

   c. Influence of Jungle Terrain on Patrolling. Many conditions of the jungle affect patrolling actions. These influencing factors, which have been previously mentioned and described are vegetation, climate, weather, terrain, and animal life. This combination of factors and elements severely limit the range, speed, and extent of patrol actions.

   (1) *Advantages.* In spite of the general hostile nature of these factors some advantages are offered. The dense vegetation affords excellent concealment and some cover which tends to favor the patrolling unit. The dense vegetation and terrain obstacles will also hinder enemy movement and observation. Advantage can also be taken of the elements, such as rain which covers the sound of movement by its own noise, or the dampness of ground and vegetation which also muffles noise of movement.

   (2) *Disadvantages.* Primary among disadvantages brought on by the influencing factors is the problem of control and movement. All movements by troop elements in the jungle must be considered tactical movements. The ease with which enemy elements can infiltrate deep into supposedly "friendly" areas, require that no relaxation into "administrative" conditions or situations be permitted once troops start a tactical exercise. This requires extensive control measures that must be effected by all leaders. Rate of movement in primary and secondary jungles is seldom more than one half mile or one kilometer each hour. Troops must be conditioned to this fact and must be trained not to overestimate the distance actually traveled. Occasionally there are small clearings where the overhead branches of trees are not thick. It is possible to receive air drops in these clearings provided adequate air-ground signals are available. Patrol leaders should attempt to accurately locate cleared areas on the map for later aerial resupply sites or medical evacuations. It would appear that because of the shade provided by trees, movement in the jungle could be made over reasonable distances without great physical discomfort from heat; however, the high humidity and the heat from the ground magnify the sensation of heat. The combination tends to exhaust troops quickly and lessens their normal powers of endurance. Owing to the restricted visibility in the jungle the only sure means to maintain direction is by compass. Every leader down to the most junior must be able to use the compass with confidence and accuracy. Movement through swamps is the most tiring and slowest of the conditions likely to be encountered.

   (3) *Minimizing the effects of the influencing factors.* Troops must be trained to pace themselves to the limitations imposed upon patrol actions by the

jungle; they must be trained to feel at home in the environment and made to realize that the jungle provides good cover and concealment which may enable them to close unobserved with the enemy and destroy them more easily.

d. Movement of Patrols in the Jungle.

(1) *Silence.* Silence, with respect to both voice and movement, is essential at all times. With practice it is possible for troops to move at a good speed in comparative silence. Each soldier should move steadily, deliberately, and carefully, parting the undergrowth rather than crashing through; attention should be given in training to correcting and eliminating the tendency of some to blunder forward. This mistake not only causes bruises, scratches, and loss of direction but is also very noisy. Troops must be taught not to walk on dry leaves, sticks, rotten wood, etc., wherever this is possible.

(2) *Cutting trail.* Troops should use their machetes to cut trail only as a last resort or to avoid excessive detours. There is nearly always a route or way nearby where movement will be easier. Cutting a trail has the following disadvantages:

(a) It is not silent.

(b) It reduces speed of movement.

(c) Fatigue of soldiers in the leading element is increased.

(d) Quick handling of weapons is prevented.

(e) It leaves a well marked trail.

(3) *Trails and trail discipline.* Movements on trails should be avoided; however, it may sometimes be necessary when speed is essential or when moving in mountainous country. Not only should patrols avoid established trails but should make all possible effort to hide signs of movement to prevent leaving a trail themselves; this is extremely important when moving through virgin country. Some aids to practice in training are:

(a) All troops should wear the same pattern sole on the combat boot.

(b) The last man in a column should brush the path made by the other members with a small branch after the patrol has passed to smooth it out or make it look as natural as possible.

(c) Troops must be required to observe trail discipline. They must NOT signpost the route with litter and waste food; these should be buried carefully. Troops on patrol should be permitted to have only the barest essentials and the minimum of comfort items when operating. Leaders must be constantly alert to prevent men from plucking leaves or breaking twigs, especially at breaks.

(d) When patrols move through close, hilly country, troops should avoid small saplings. The shaking of overhead branches can be seen and heard at a distance.

(e) When moving through tree cultivations, patrol members must keep off trails, if only by walking a few feet off these trails.

(4) *Speed of movement.* The general restrictions on movement indicated by paragraph 10 of this manual apply in the instances of patrols. However, because patrols usually must operate according to a most stringent time schedule some discussion of this facet of operations is considered appropriate. Speed of movement is dictated by the nature of the country, the mission, and the schedule previously mentioned. Speed in moving from one location to another will be better obtained by intelligent route planning than by trying to push quickly and blindly forward. It is important to emphasize in training that speed will always be limited by the necessity to avoid noise in movement; also, movement must be expected to be painfully slow. Movement in the jungle is fatiguing, both physically and mentally, and a balance between the desire to move quickly must be maintained with the necessity of keeping troops fresh, strong, and alert for action once the objective is reached. Halts must be called for observation and listening and less frequently for rest. In training there should be no set routine for rest breaks. If these rest periods are allowed at regular intervals, troops may look forward and concentrate on the anticipated halts to the exclusion of all other considerations. Terrain difficulties will usually dictate when to take breaks. It must be emphasized in training that all members of a patrol must concentrate with all their senses to the task at hand; the jungle is no place for allowing the mind to wander or to allow the soldier to be preoccupied with his own discomforts. When halted, troops must always take up positions providing for all around security. When marching in single file it may be necessary to delegate responsibility for protection and lookouts down to groups. As a guide, it is suggested that, when working out times for rest halts, the patrol leader consider the ground over which the unit is moving. In relatively easy terrain he should start with the usual ten minutes in the hour for rest breaks; under such conditions he should not march for longer periods as the men may resent this. However, when traversing difficult country halts must be more frequent; only a patrol leader who knows the physical condition of his men can determine how frequent these halts should be. After passing through a swamp or climbing a steep slope, it is a good plan to call a short break. It is important that the patrol leader ascertain that the entire patrol has passed through a defile, cleared a swamp, or ascended a steep slope to relatively level ground before ordering a halt. If this is not done, only the leading elements will be rested. Of more serious consequence will be the detrimental effect on morale; the

men to the rear will have serious doubts about the patrol leader's concern for their welfare if they experience many "rest breaks" in swamps, steep slopes, ant-infested clearings, prickly saw-tooth grass patches, or other poor sites.

(5) *Observation.* A soldier must notice every sign of movement around him, all marks or signs on the ground, and all instances of broken, cut or trampled vegetation. The sense of smell must be keen and free from cigarette smoke, the odor of candy, the smell of hair oil, shave lotion, or talcum so that the individual soldier will immediately notice any strange smells. All of these unnecessary Items should be denied troops in training to illustrate the detrimental effects they can produce. Periodically, depending on how close the patrol leader suspects the enemy to be, the patrol should stop and listen. At halts, every member of the patrol concentrates on listening and reports anything he hears. Troops must be trained to disregard the general pattern of foliage immediately surrounding them and to look "through" rather than "at" the vegetation. A better view is often obtained by looking through jungle at ground level. If any unusual sign or sound is noted a patrol must "freeze" in place silently; there should be no other movement until the patrol leader has investigated the situation.

e. Control Measures. It is obvious that when confronted with the many problems presented by the jungle a patrol leader must concern himself with the means to control his force. Voice commands are of limited effectiveness and are a threat to secrecy; other audible signals suffer from the same disadvantages. The most effective control means available to a patrol leader are silent arm and hand signals. A number of these signals has been discussed previously. Any number or combination of signals to denote specific meanings may be developed within units. It must be remembered, however, that signals must be kept to a minimum commensurate with the needs of a patrol and that once a standard pattern is adopted it must be practiced in training situations or rehearsed until the entire code is understood by all members of a unit or a selected patrolling force.

(1) *Formations.*

(a) Squad. Generally, two types of formations for squad-sized patrols will suffice for movement in the jungle. These are the single file and open formations; these are similar to the "column" and V formations used in more open terrain.

(b) Platoon. The squads of a platoon will usually have to move in file or column formation in the jungle. At times the nature of the terrain may require a more open formation; in this case rifle squads may move, two or three forward, on parallel axes. The patrol leader must constantly analyze the ground and vary formations of the patrol to suit it.

(2) *Position of leaders.* Squad leaders should remain with and control their squads. This can usually be done from near the head of the column; maximum use should be made of fire team leaders to maintain control and man-to-man contact with squad members. Leaders of platoon-sized or commanders of company-sized patrols will be located within their patrols according to the dictates of the ground, the tactical situation and the formation used. These positions should be sufficiently far forward to—

(a) Allow the leader to influence the action from the start. Although it is not desirable for the leader to be caught in opening bursts of fire he should place himself where he can direct and quickly exploit immediate action drills.

(b) Enable the leader to exercise and enforce control measures, control the point and navigation team, read the map, and order halts properly when deemed necessary.

(3) *Guides.* The word "guide" is used here as denoting someone with an intimate knowledge of an area or anyone who can lead friendly forces to a known enemy location. These may be surrendered enemy personnel, captured enemy personnel, or natives. Information received from any of these sources should be carefully evaluated and used with reservation. It is unwise to completely depend upon all information offered by "friendly" natives or enemy personnel. If patrol leaders are not careful, there will be a tendency to allow guides to lead a patrol. This is most certainly wrong because—

(a) They are not trained scouts and are not part of the military team. Their function, if reliable, is merely to show direction.

(b) If enemy troops are encountered en route, guides may panic and prejudice the patrol's chances of accomplishing the mission.

(c) Patrol leaders must be ever wary of being led into an ambush by treacherous and seemingly well-meaning guides. The correct position of a guide, if used on a patrol, is with the patrol leader. The patrol leader will make decisions as to direction and tactics, using the guide's advice as he deems appropriate,

(4) *Maintaining contact.* The patrol leader must always adapt his speed of movement to that of his rear elements; in other words, responsibility for keeping touch must be from front to rear. The flanks or flank security must maintain their position by the center of the column. The only exception to this rule will be the lead element whose whole attention must be focused forward.

41. Ambush

a. General. In no other type of military operation is the ambush more important, more effective or more frequently employed than in jungle combat. An ambush is a specialized form of combat in which the principles of concealment, surprise, and offensive action are used to inflict maximum casualties, confusion, and destruction to any enemy on the move. Since the ambush does not require the seizure and holding of ground, it is a favorite tactic of the guerrilla who will make every effort to infiltrate the jungle for purposes of ambush. The basic elements of ambush are covered in other publications such as FM 21-50, FM 21-75 and FM 31-16. However, because of their application in jungle operations a detailed discussion of this subject is included.

b. Role of the Individual Soldier in an Ambush. The individual soldier must be impressed with the fact that he alone is the key element in an ambush. In the jungle, his self-discipline and readiness will be a deciding factor in success or failure.

c. Ambush. Ambush may be defined as: "A trap sprung on a moving or temporarily halted enemy column and is based on concentrated surprise fire from concealed positions." Special note should be taken of the words "trap" and "sprung" and the phrases "concentrated SURPRISE fire" and "concealed positions". A trap is "sprung" because it moves suddenly, rapidly, and without warning. The fires of weapons are "concentrated" because the target area is small and the volume of delivered fire is of great intensity; these fires can be directed at a single point or small area because the delivery is made suddenly, violently, and without prior indication. "Concealed positions" prevent members of the ambush and their equipment from being seen by the enemy. This is the absolute requirement of ambush, for without concealment there is no surprise and without surprise there is no successful ambush, and an unsuccessful ambush is frequently fatal to those who fail.

d. Purposes of Ambush. Generally, ambushes are executed to reduce the enemy's combat effectiveness by the physical damage caused and through the harassment involved.

(1) *Means to accomplish these purposes.*

(*a*) Destruction is the primary purpose, because loss of men and equipment critically affects the enemy. He will have to divert troops from other missions to protect himself against ambush. The failure of reconnaissance and combat patrols to accomplish their missions because they were ambushed deprives the enemy of valuable contributions these patrols would make to his combat efforts.

(*b*) The damage caused by the harassment of frequent ambushes is less apparent than physical damage, but is very important. When ambushes are frequent, troops tend to be reluctant to go on patrols, move in convoys, and move in small groups. They become less aggressive and more defensive minded; they avoid night operations, become more subject to confusion and panic if ambushed, and, in general, decline in effectiveness.

(c) An ambush may be an ideal method to obtain intelligence. A successful ambush enables us to capture prisoners, documents, and pieces of ordnance, make identification of enemy units by observing insignia on dead or captured soldiers, give us indications of enemy combat proficiency level by their reactions to ambush and give us information on the status of combat equipage. The extent of the enemy's familiarity with the terrain may also be revealed by his actions.

(d) Patrols operating deep in enemy areas may be able to partially or completely resupply themselves through ambushes set to seize supplies and equipment, thus increasing combat effectiveness at the expense of the enemy. In many instances, this is the primary source of supplies and materiel for guerrilla elements.

e. Characteristics of Ambush.

(1) *Surprise.* The most important element of an ambush is surprise. If surprise is not achieved there is no ambush. It is the decisive factor which shifts the immediate control of the combat situation to the ambushing force. It consists of striking the enemy when, where and in a manner for which he is unprepared. If the enemy cannot be taken completely by surprise, he must become aware too late to react effectively. Surprise can be achieved by speed, secrecy, deception, by variation in means and methods and by using seemingly impossible terrain. Effective firepower must exploit surprise.

(2) *Control.* Control is difficult to establish and maintain. Control is necessary during the movement to, occupation of, and withdrawal from the ambush site. The most crucial time of the ambush operation is the moment the enemy arrives at the site. Control measures must be provided for opening fire. The time the enemy's lead element arrives at a certain location may be designated as the time to open fire. In any event, opening fires must be in direct control of the ambush commander. Communications with security elements is essential and with higher headquarters is desirable. Exacting control must be exercised to insure that the ambushing force is alert and silent. Assembly and rallying points are designated to assist in control during withdrawal.

(3) *Concentrated fires.* The short killing time demands highly concentrated fires which are achieved by careful planning and positioning of weapons. The fires of all weapons, including rifles, close-in automatic weapons, rocket launchers, grenade launchers, claymore mines, and other weapons are tied

into the fire plan. The assignment of sectors of fire, and the location of friendly elements are considered. Plans are made for isolating the ambush area to prevent escape and reinforcement by the enemy. Effectiveness of the ambush depends upon the surprise delivery of a large volume of fire. Fire from at least two directions and converging on the target is desirable; care must be exercised to prevent friendly troops from firing into other friendly positions of the ambush when converging fire is used.

(4) *Simplicity.* Another essential characteristic of the ambush is simplicity. Simple plans and orders are easily understood and executed, particularly if the ambush is to be in position for a long period of time; lengthy detailed orders are not likely to be remembered exactly and consequently, are either not carried out or are misinterpreted. This may occur even after detailed rehearsals.

(5) *Concentration of action.* Once sprung, an ambush must use all available firepower. To do this requires careful attention during training. Under excitement some men will shoot ineffectively, or fail to fire their weapons. In addition, due to the limited zone of fire, some of the enemy may escape the initial fire. This can be overcome by a determined assault against the enemy by all or part of the ambush patrol.

(6) *Discipline.* The last characteristic is self-discipline. Remaining in a set ambush can be a boring and uncomfortable job. It may be necessary for the soldier to forego smoking; to endure in silence, insect bites, thirst, and the desire to ease cramped legs, or to perform normal body functions. Systematic and continuous training is necessary to develop the required patience and self-discipline.

f. Factors of the Successful Ambush. There are several considerations or factors that affect the constitution of a successful ambush. These factors are:

(1) *Plan.* The plan for an ambush (deliberate) must provide for every conceivable course of action the enemy is capable of adopting and must be rehearsed in detail. Tentative plans must be made for ambushes of opportunity, adopting or modifying as appropriate, at the ambush site. The plan must provide for—

(a) Ease and completeness of expression by operations order.

(b) Deployment—ambush formations to be used.

(c) Organization and size of ambush.

(d) Type of ambush.

(e) Equipment to be taken.

(f) Actions to be taken.

(g) Routes to be followed.

(h) Formations on the march.

1. When developing the plan, it must be kept simple to eliminate confusion. If one man forgets what he is supposed to do, the entire ambush is endangered.

2. The next consideration is the equipment to be taken. Special equipment might be needed above that which the men of the patrol are normally equipped. Examples are: infrared equipment, mines, demolitions, sound-powered telephones, ropes and gags for prisoners, and extra machineguns or automatic rifles.

3. Routes are carefully selected. A good patrol leader avoids danger areas, such as roads, bridges, fords, known enemy locations, civilians, and villages. Generally, the patrol should not use the same route back as it used on its trip to the ambush site.

4. Another important element of the plan is the formation to be used. Only basic formations should be prescribed. One formation is the single flanking force which requires that the patrol be placed along the side of the area to be ambushed. The advantage of this formation is its ease of control, and the use of but one rallying point. Disadvantages lie in the fact that the enemy may escape from the ambush patrol and the lateral dispersion of a large force might be too great for effective coverage. Another formation is the single flanking force with a decoy. The decoy may be a piece of equipment or other item that will attract the attention of the enemy soldiers causing them to bunch up. When the enemy is gathered around the decoy, the patrol open fire, killing as many of the enemy as possible in the opening volley. The formation has all the advantages of the single flanking force; however, there is the disadvantage that the attempt at ruse may become apparent and alert the enemy. Another formation that may be prescribed within the plan is the L formation and its companion the V formation. In these formations, the patrol is split into two groups, one group is placed alongside the trail while the other group is perpendicular to the trail; in the V formation, the apex of the V meets at the trail and the patrol is disposed laterally along both sides of the trail, making sure that one group does not fire into the other. The advantages of these formations are that the enemy is caught in a cross-fire and fewer escape routes are available to him. Disadvantages are found in that control is difficult because the patrol is split, two routes of withdrawal and additional rally points are usually required and there are fewer sites that favor these formations.

5. The plan must provide for the organization and size of the ambush patrol. Determining factors here are the purpose of the ambush, the enemy force to be attacked and the personnel, weapons, and equipment available.

6. The general type of ambush must be determined and be stated in the plan. The deliberate ambush is executed when prior information of the targets permits detailed planning before the patrol departs for the ambush site. Likely targets would be: any enemy force, when prior information is known; enemy patrols operating on a pattern of times and routes; or carrying parties moving on patterned routes and time schedules. A hasty ambush would be used when available information does not allow detailed planning prior to departure of the patrol. There are several courses of action to govern conduct of such an ambush patrol. Immediate reconnoitering of a suitable ambush area could be made allowing execution against the first target of opportunity. Or, such a patrol could depart after dark, ambush the first target of opportunity and return before daylight. Such a patrol can also ambush an enemy element in a situation in which contact cannot be avoided.

(2) *Site.* When siting an ambush the terrain must be carefully analyzed. A careful study must be made using maps, aerial photographs, and when possible, a personal reconnaissance. The ground must enable occupation and/or preparation of concealed positions. All reconnaissance and movement into position must be from the rear of the selected ambush position. Covered routes of withdrawal should be available to enable the ambush to break contact and avoid pursuit by fire. Favorable fields (tunnels) of fire must be allowed the ambush. The site selected should impose canalization of the enemy force into the killing zone; the site should, of course, afford a position insuring contact with the enemy. The site must contribute to, or at least not detract from, the surprise of the ambush. Considering this, the ambush patrol leader does not have to select the best ground or terrain suited tactically for his ambush. Many times the selection of a site for surprise alone will be more advantageous than attempting to ambush an enemy from a spot of which he is sure to be suspicious. Therefore, the ambush might be laid downhill from the enemy as well as uphill. When downhill from the enemy, it becomes more difficult for him to escape since he will have to escape uphill. If the ambush is uphill from the enemy, it is easier for him to escape by running downhill. However, if advantage is taken of natural obstacles or mines, the uphill position should be the more successful of the two.

(3) *Positions.* When the patrol reaches the site, the patrol leader first places his security force out to prevent being surprised while positioning his ambush

force proper. The next elements to go into position are the automatic weapons. These positions are selected so they can allow fire along the entire killing zone. If this is not possible, these weapons are given overlapping sectors of fire, making sure the entire killing zone is covered by automatic weapons fire. After the automatic weapons are positioned the patrol leader selects his position. He should be located at the point in the ambush where he can tell when the proper time comes to commence firing. After he has selected his position, he or his assistants place the riflemen in position. The riflemen are placed so they can cover any dead space left by the automatic weapons. Positioning of weapons should allow mutual support by assignment of sectors of fire.

(4) *Camouflage.* Camouflage plays an important role in the ambush. The aim of the ambush is to kill the enemy by surprising him, and to do this each member of the ambush patrol must be hidden from the enemy's view. Before moving out each patrol member camouflages his person and his equipment; he also tightens his equipment to prevent rattles. After going into position he carefully conceals himself to prevent being seen. Lastly, there must be no unnecessary talking, smoking, or movement. If reliefs are to be used, they should be prearranged. Once the relief begins, only a few men should move at a time, because it is less likely that one or two men moving at once will be spotted, whereas if the entire relief moved at once, the chances of being seen would become much greater. In no other operation is camouflage discipline more important than in the ambush. Weapons should fire through screens of undisturbed, living foliage, and all spoilage resulting from preparation of positions should be removed.

(5) *Signals.* An ambush patrol leader will need at least three signals for his ambush: a warning signal, a signal for execution, and a signal for withdrawal. The warning signal should be a silent signal. Examples of silent signals are hand and arm signals and vines or cords laid across the arms of selected members of the patrol. When the enemy comes into sight the sentry pulls on the vine causing it to move across the arm of the patrol leader. He in turn alerts the other members of the patrol. The signal for execution may be the exploding of mines, or it may be a shot fired by the ambush patrol leader or his assistant. Other signals are rapping or snapping sounds such as hitting the helmet with a stone, hitting two metal objects together, or the breaking of a stick. For the signal to withdraw, voice commands, whistles or pyrotechnics may be used. The signals should be changed frequently so as not to compromise them.

(6) *Fire discipline.* A key part of the ambush, in effective execution, is fire discipline. The timing and delivery of fires must contribute not only to surprise but to the actual destruction of the enemy. This requires control,

and the patrol leader exercises this control by assigning sectors of fire and by commands.

(7) *Withdrawal.* Before the withdrawal begins, several actions might have taken place. First, the patrol was successful and destroyed the enemy forces, or accomplished its assigned mission thereby eliminating any immediate danger to itself. In that case the patrol leader would move his patrol back to the rallying point, complete any necessary reorganization, and return to friendly lines quickly but carefully. If one of the patrol's missions was to search the dead for documents, seize equipment, or take prisoners, that portion of the patrol assigned this task would carry it out while the other members of the patrol would cover them. Then the patrol would withdraw the same as in the first example. If the patrol could not overcome the enemy column, it would become necessary for the patrol to immediately withdraw and move with deliberate speed to the rally point, quickly reorganize, and depart the area. Regardless of what happens, on receiving the signal to withdraw the assault element moves along a previously reconnoitered path to the rally point. Situation permitting, each member of the patrol selects a route to the rally point and walks his route until he can follow it even

Soldiers of the 173rd Airborne Brigade in a firefight on Hill 823, 1967.

in the dark. The rally point should be far enough from the ambush site so that there is no danger of its being over-run if the enemy attacks the ambush. At the rally point, the patrol is checked for missing members and casualties, then moves on its return march. Mines can be pre-located on the side of the withdrawal route and when the patrol withdraws they can be armed to impede the enemy's pursuit.

g. Defense Against Ambush. In planning for defense, the planner must initially consider the friendly forces available. The small unit commander responsible for moving a unit independently through areas where ambush is likely must plan for the formation to be used, march security, communications and control, special equipment, the actions to be taken if ambushed, and the reorganization.

(1) *Formation.* A formation which provides all-around security is always desirable. However, any formation used should provide security to the unit. In the jungle, troops usually move in a column or file. This is necessary for control purposes due to the dense undergrowth. This growth hinders but does not preclude the use of a point, flank guards, and rear guard. The interval between men should be about 5 yards where visibility permits. The commander should be well forward in the column and the firepower of the unit should be evenly dispersed throughout the column. Then, if ambushed, all of his firepower, machineguns and other major weapons are not knocked out in the initial burst.

(2) *Security.* Regardless of the formation employed, security to the front, rear, and flanks is necessary when ambush is likely and, in the jungle, ambush is always likely. A front security element should provide its own flank security, be placed well forward or as far forward as possible and still be in communication with the main body. The front security element must be strong enough to sustain itself until followup units can be deployed to assist in reducing the ambush. Flank security elements in the jungle usually must move adjacent to the column along routes paralleling the direction of march. The flank security elements must, however, be close enough for control and yet distant enough to preclude jeopardy to the main column in the event it receives fire. Rear security elements perform similarly to the point; it can be used as a maneuver element in the event of ambush.

(3) *Control.* The use of communications equipment and control measures are the next items the commander considers. All available means of communications are used to assist in maintaining control. In addition, detailed prior planning, briefings, and rehearsals for all personnel will assist if an ambush does occur. It must be remembered that in the jungle there is no substitute for personal contact effected by the patrol leader with his subordinates to insure maximum control of his force.

(4) *Special equipment.* Additional items of equipment and weapons are sometimes needed by a unit, especially when it moves through areas where guerrillas are likely to be encountered. Additional automatic weapons may be necessary; pioneer tools and mine detectors are used to detect and reduce roadblocks or minefields. Demolition equipment is used to destroy obstacles encountered en route. Additional communications equipment and identification devices such as panel sets, lights, or smoke grenades may be required.

(5) *Reaction to ambush.* The most effective means of combating an ambush is to prevent this action from being launched against the unit. This is accomplished by constant and correct employment of security. Once ambush is initiated against the column, all weapons must immediately return the fire. This requires discipline, dynamic leadership, and rehearsed plans. Elements must then be made aware that an assault must take place despite the fact that the unit may have suffered heavy casualties. A retrograde movement in lieu of an assault may, in a well-prepared ambush, result in complete annihilation of the friendly unit. Reorganization after an ambush involves the use of rallying points, plans for local security, reconstitution of depleted patrol elements, evacuation of casualties, and further movement based on the unit mission.

42. Counterambush

a. Dismounted Troops. Counterambush techniques to be employed by dismounted troops when ambushed are called "immediate action" drills. They apply for use immediately before the unit leader or commander has time to issue any detailed orders. The sudden enemy action in an ambush demands immediate, preplanned reaction.

b. Mounted Troops. Roads are extremely scarce in jungle areas. In some locations, however, the jungle edge is adjacent to roads, making ambush of vehicular columns extremely easy; units must consider the danger of ambush ever present in such areas regardless of the tactical or administrative situation. Although ambush of vehicular columns is a primary tactic of guerrillas, it must be expected that conventional enemy forces will employ this technique whenever possible. When considering a plan for training of troops in countering enemy actions, if attacked while moving in vehicles two things should be borne in mind. First, the opportunity must be taken to inflict maximum casualties upon the enemy by attack and the resulting action should not be looked upon as a retaliatory measure only. Second, the purpose of guerrillas staging an ambush of a vehicular column is primarily to gain arms, ammunition, and food; consequently, every effort must be expended to prevent these vital supplies from falling into their hands to include deliberate booby trapping.

(1) *Typical ambush pattern against motorized elements.*

(a) Obviously military vehicles will be the primary targets of road ambushes. However, civilian vehicles may be fired upon for propaganda purposes or to create obstacles.

(b) Most roads in jungle areas run through country offering covered lines of approach and withdrawal and affording covered positions from which to fire on vehicles. Enemy forces therefore can be expected to select that part of a road where it would be easy to place a roadblock or where vehicles would have to move slowly, such as a climb into a cut a sharp bend, or a climbing turn.

(c) Enemy forces can be expected to accept a risk of remaining concentrated at a certain locale for extended periods in order to ambush a lucrative target.

(d) Ambush of motorized elements must be expected at night. Enemy forces will be able to deploy greater fire power using fewer troops because of the ease of concealment afforded by darkness. Some forms of night ambushes might be:

1. Fairly heavy sniping fire from different locations within the ambush position at the vehicles in a column.

2. Deliberate ambush of a convoy based on exact information obtained through intelligence.

3. Deliberate ambush of a particular vehicle or vehicles.

(2) *Countering road ambushes.* There are two ways to prevent or minimize the incidence of ambush on roads. These are:

(a) Precautionary measures to reduce chances of being ambushed and to insure instant readiness for action.

(b) Actions on contact, or immediate action drills, designed to gain the initiative by offensive action.

(3) *Precautionary measures.* All roads should be classified into categories with the classification being based primarily on estimated enemy action in the areas concerned. Traffic on all roads in combat areas must be rigidly controlled and kept to a minimum. All vehicles must have at least one armed rider as air guard, travel at night must be heavily restricted, use of armored vehicles must be increased with convoys, and information relating to convoy or vehicle movements must be carefully guarded. Every unit should formulate comprehensive standing operating procedures covering movement by roads. This SOP should state clearly who is authorized to put a convoy on the road and should also provide, in detail, information concerning the appointment and duties or convoy and vehicle commanders, the organization of convoys,

weapons and basic loads to be carried, instructions regarding windshields, tailgates and tarpaulins of vehicles, stipulated immediate action drills, and instructions to describe security policies. This SOP must be rehearsed in training until all troops respond effectively.

(4) *Actions on contact.* An ambush will always be an unexpected encounter. The only solution to this event is correct and timely reaction of troops. A road ambush will be carefully chosen and converted into a position from which fire from above and at point-blank range can be delivered on a convoy. The principle behind immediate action drills is that it is incorrect to halt in the killing zone unless forced to do so. Drills, then, should teach troops to drive on when fired upon, to halt only when through the ambush killing zone or before running into it and to counterattack immediately from flank and rear.

(a) Immediate action techniques. Every effort should be made to get vehicles clear of the killing zone when fire is received. Thus, when vehicles are fired upon:

1. Drivers should not stop but should attempt to drive on until out of the apparent killing zone.

2. Lookout men (three or four to each troop-carrying vehicle) will fire immediately upon the ambush.

3. If vehicles are clear of the killing zone they will be stopped to allow occupants to detruck to carry out offensive actions.

4. Vehicles approaching the killing zone should not attempt to run through the ambush; rather, they should halt clear of the area and discharge occupants for deployment.

5. Drivers will be key men and should be selected accordingly.

(b) Counterattack. Ambush positions are vulnerable at their rear and flanks. Offensive actions normally can be carried out only by troops who are clear of the killing zone. If there are no such troops, then a frontal attack under concealment of smoke will be necessary. Some conditions under which counterattacks will be made are:

1. When no troops have entered the killing zone. The convoy commander or, in his absence the senior vehicle commander present, should launch an immediate flanking attack on the ambush position. All available crew-served weapons should bring supporting fires to bear on the ambush.

2. When all troops are clear ahead of the danger zone. An attack under this condition is liable to be delayed as troops might be moving away from the place of the ambush. Nevertheless, an encircling attack

must be organized and launched as soon as troops can concentrate. Who commands and which elements will take the initiative in these circumstances must be spelled out in the unit SOP or other instructions.

3. When some troops are clear ahead of the killing zone and others are halted short of it. With two troop elements on both sides of an ambush, separated by a killing zone, confusion may arise as to which group should attack and, as a consequence, valuable time may be wasted. If both elements attack at the same time without prior coordination, an interunit clash may result.

4. When armor is available. Usually the best way in which an armored vehicle could assist in counterambush would be to drive directly into the killing zone and engage the ambush at point-blank range. This would give good covering fire to the flanking attack made by foot troops and afford some protection to friendly troops caught in the killing zone.

5. When the convoy commander becomes a casualty. Since it is possible that the convoy commander might be killed, wounded, or pinned down in the killing zone, it is essential that all vehicle commanders know their responsibilities for conducting a counterattack. This should be clearly given in unit convoy orders, SOP, or briefings before a convoy moves on a road.

(5) *Bailing out drill.* Usually when an enemy force springs a road ambush all effort will be made to stop as many vehicles as possible in the killing zone by the use of mines or obstacles or by firing at the tires and driver of a vehicle. Therefore, it is essential that troops know how to detruck instantly. This must be taught and practiced as drill during training. The elements of this drill are:

(a) Vehicle loading. All packs and equipment should be placed in the center of the truck. Excessive quantities of equipment or other items should not be loaded into vehicles which are carrying troops. Trucks used for carrying troop should have the tarpaulins and rib bows removed. Sixteen to eighteen men should be the maximum number carried in the back of a 2½ ton truck. If more than this number are carried, they may be unable to use their weapons effectively, get in each other's way, and be difficult for the vehicle commander to control. Similarly the number of troops carried in other types of vehicles must be restricted to insure freedom of movement.

(b) Alertness. Lookouts should be posted on all four corners of the vehicles or, as a minimum, one in front and one in rear. They should be continuously alert. Other troops should be ready, but need not maintain

alert. It. will be necessary on long trips to rotate the lookouts. Spare magazines should be in pouches, not in boxes; vehicle lookouts should have grenades available for immediate throwing.

(c) Bailing out procedures. When the vehicle is forced to stop, these procedures should be followed:

1. The vehicle commander shouts "detruck right" or "detruck left" to indicate the direction in which troops will go to organize.

2. Vehicle lookouts should throw grenades and open fire immediately on the ambush position.

3. Troops should detruck over both sides and not from the rear of vehicles and run in the direction indicated by the vehicle commander.

4. As soon as troops clear the vehicle, lookouts should join those who evacuated the truck.

5. At this stage the immediate task is to collect the fit men for counteraction. Wounded soldiers must be dealt with after the action has terminated.

6. The above, and many other possible variations, should be made into SOPs and practiced until a high degree of proficiency is attained.

The following list of infantry "patrol tips" offers a fascinating window into the minutiae of infantry operations in Vietnam. The breadth and variety of the tips suggest that all are born from hard practical experience. A piece of equipment that might seem inessential before the operation can suddenly become the key to success or failure in the field. Not taking gloves, for example, would often result in torn and infected hands that if severe enough might need a medevac. The author recommends the use of scout dogs, which were not only invaluable to detecting booby traps and hidden VC, but had the added benefit of psychologically terrifying the enemy. The injunction to "Always carry weapons at the ready" was doubtless the product of sudden ambush. Each tip is a judicious insight into the small world of decisions that could make the difference between living and dying.

From "Annex D (Patrol Tips) to SOP No 1. 2d Bn, 35th Inf APO 96355, US Army, 1 Nov 1967" (1967)

1. Make a detailed map study of the terrain over which the patrol will pass. Consider selecting the most difficult terrain. Terrain is seldom impassable to a determined patrol.

2. Make a detailed reconnaissance, both ground and air if possible. Take your subordinate leaders, point and compass men whenever possible.

3. Avoid taking weapons requiring different types of ammunition.

4. Make maximum use of grenades and claymores.

5. Individual weapons cleaning equipment should be carried.

6. Carry gloves to protect hands.

7. Carry two of each critical items such as flashlights, binoculars, fuze crimpers, wire cutters, etc.

8. Carry extra batteries on long patrols. Always start with a fresh battery.

9. Carry two ponchos for map checks and to make rafts.

10. Every man should carry a pair of dry socks sealed in a waterproof plastic bag already powdered for use.

11. Consider the use of scout dogs.

12. Tape all items that might rattle.

13. Assign each man a certain area to secure during movement, halts, rally points, etc.

14. Check the camouflage of each man on the back of his hands and neck and behind his ears as well as the obvious areas. Also check the camouflage on weapons and uniforms.

15. Always use two pacers each with a small string keeping count by tying knots. Take the average.

16. Preset your compass before departing.

17. Do not mark your maps with routes, friendly areas or enemy locations.

18. Do not take SOIs or written radio frequencies with you. Memorize the information.

19. On night patrols, do not allow cigarettes or matches to be carried. This reduces temptation.

20. Prepare a checklist for coordination at friendly positions through which you must pass.

21. Use field expedient radio antennas when greater range is required.

22. Carry several short lengths of rope for POWs and one 50' length to assist in crossing streams.

23. Carry a small grappling hook to dislodge items that may be boobytrapped.

24. Two pieces of luminous tape (½" by ½") on the rear of the collar or hat will greatly aid in movement on dark nights.

25. Clean, check and test fire all weapons before departing on the rehearsal.

26. Check all equipment for proper functioning prior to moving out for the rehearsal.

27. Always use a sketch or terrain board in issuing your patrol order.

28. Prearrange and rehearse all signals. Keep signals simple.

29. Allow time for patrol member's eyes to become "dark adapted" before departing, normally ½ hour.

30. Explain the terrain of the actual ambush site to the patrol at the rehearsal site when conducting the first "walk through" rehearsal.

31. Inspect your patrol in detail. Question every man on his job and the patrol actions planned.

32. Send up the count after each halt or passage of a danger area.

33. Designate rallying points frequently and at easy to find locations.

34. Use the point man <u>only</u> for security to the front. Make another man the compass man.

35. Check navigation frequently. Use your compass every 15 minutes or so. Keep your own pace as a double check.

36. On long patrols or in difficult terrain change point and compass men occasionally.

37. Use the battalion password only when meeting other patrols. Use your own password within the patrol or use a number recognition system.

38. Stay off roads and trails.

39. Avoid villages and hamlets. The dogs always give you away.

40. Avoid all danger areas.

41. Take advantage of battle noise and natural noise when moving.

42. Call for artillery in a distant area to cover your movement noise.

43. Fire artillery near your location every so often to give the appearance of H and Is [Harassment and Interdiction fire].

Members of Companies B and D, 1st Battalion, 501st Infantry, Regiment, 101st Airborne Division, rest up during operations in June 1969.

44. Do not move along ridge tops either during daylight or darkness. You may use the military crest because movement is easier but you must stay off the skyline.

45. Always carry all weapons at the ready.

46. Cut or disturb wire only after you are sure it is not boobytrapped.

47. The compass can be used for signaling over short distances providing the luminous dial is charged by light.

48. Know your location at all times and report it frequently. Prearrange reports with your next senior headquarters to keep radio transmission time and talking to a minimum.

49. Cross roads, streams and open areas only after a reconnaissance has been made of the other side and security is established.

50. Always have the entire patrol ready to support by fire before sending out a reconnaissance element to check the opposite side of a rice paddy.

51. Always bury all trash and camouflage the hole.

52. Prearrange some artillery concentrations along the route to be used as navigational aids.

53. Break contact with the enemy by the "clock system" and fire and movement or by an immediate action drill.

54. Do not talk on patrols. Whisper, and do that only when necessary. Use hand and arm signals whenever possible.

55. When "passing up the word" do not change a single word of the message. Repeat exactly what you were told.

56. Always follow the patrol order format when issuing the order. It will help you cover all points.

57. At rehearsal insist that every man do exactly as he would on patrol.

58. Make every man carry all of his patrol equipment to rehearsal and insure that he is carrying the correct equipment.

59. The rehearsal is the most important part of preparation. Demand it be executed correctly. Repeat it until the action is perfected.

60. Do not allow the patrol to eat their final meal until the rehearsal and inspection have been completed satisfactorily.

61. Carry a spare handset for the radio in a waterproof bag.

The Vietnam War, and the diligent efforts of archivists, has left us with a vast archive of U.S. Army infantry after-action reports, many of which conclude with a "lessons learned" section that summarized the tactical knowledge acquired from the particular operation. The following report was part of a broader compilation of these reports. The explanatory document that introduces the report explains that it "is the first of the 1968 special series of numbered Operations Reports – Lessons Learned. It contains a summary of selected items based on information reported in Operational Reports – Lessons Learned and Combat After Action reports submitted during 1967." Information collected in documents such as these would be distributed to frontline units and training formations back in the States, hopefully to improve the survivability of those new to Vietnam operations. In the extracts below, there are interesting discussions about various tactical challenges, particularly those relating to winkling out the enemy from rocky cave complexes (common in mountainous areas). On a similar theme, the document that then follows focuses on the nerve-shredding activity of neutralizing enemy tunnel systems. It was developed by one Major Ben G. Crosby of the 2nd Battalion, 35th Infantry, and was considered of such value that it was published by the HQ of Military Assistance Command, Vietnam (MACV) in December 1968.

From "Operations Report—Lessons Learned 1-68: Summary of Lessons" (1968)

SECTION 1
MANEUVER TACTICS AND TECHNIQUES

1. ITEM: Pursuit, battlefield sweep and evacuation of the wounded. (670698)

DISCUSSION: The 4th Infantry Division reports that there is a built-in conflict as to what action should be taken immediately upon the enemy attempting to withdraw in the dense jungle near the Cambodian Border. The ideal situation would be to have a landing zone in the immediate proximity of the contact area through which reinforcements could be inserted to initiate an aggressive exploitation or pursuit. Simultaneously, the US unit in contact should evacuate its wounded and dead and initiate an immediate sweep of the battlefield. However, in dense jungle landing zones are not readily available in the vast majority of cases. As soon as the situation permits, and in the absence of a landing zone, the US unit must cut a landing zone out of the jungle foliage to evacuate the wounded. The normal time required to cut such a landing zone is about 15 hours, but may often extend to 24 hours and, on occasion, may exceed 36 hours. During this period, the enemy is making a maximum effort to evacuate his wounded, documents, weapons and other items of equipment from the battle area. In many cases, he is able to physically remove his dead before a sweep of the battlefield can be accomplished.

OBSERVATION: Each situation must be analyzed carefully to determine the sequence of the actions to be taken. If at all possible, reinforcements should be inserted to pursue the enemy and to otherwise exploit the situation. Moreover, immediate action must be taken either by the US unit in contact or by the reinforcing unit, as the case may be, to conduct an immediate sweep of the battlefield. Obviously, the seriously wounded must be evacuated from the battlefield by the fastest method in order to prevent further loss of lives. To accomplish all of these things in the proper order or simultaneously requires careful judgment and coordination by the commanders involved.

2. ITEM: Combat in rock complexes. (67X071)

DISCUSSION: The 3d Brigade, 25th Infantry Division, during Operation Thayer II, conducted sustained combat operations in mountainous terrain containing numerous rock complexes. The following is based on the brigade's experiences:

a. Operations within rock complexes. Combating the enemy within a cave is extremely difficult. Since the enemy inhabits the cave, he knows where the passages lead and has the advantage of interior lines of communication in his reinforcing capability. Additionally, he has a defense plan based on a detailed reconnaissance, knowing well in advance what avenues of approach must be used by his opponents. The attacker has no way to make a reconnaissance except by fire. Although the advantage is on defense, there are several advantages that accrue to the attacker. The attacker has the initiative and freedom to choose where and when to strike. Secondly, the attacker has a significant psychological advantage in that the defender harbors a great fear of being entombed alive. The final result depends mostly on the quality of the individuals fighting the engagement.

b. Organization of rock complex fighting teams. A typical rock complex fighting team consists of three to four men led by an experienced non-commissioned officer. The point man leads the way and provides security to the front. The second man in line, normally the leader, provides observation and security to the flanks. The rear man secures the rear and becomes the guide in case a rapid withdrawal is necessary. The point man should carry a large flashlight to investigate cracks and crevices. This light must be cautiously used as it will often draw enemy fire. Training and practice in the attack of a rock complex are absolute necessities for successful accomplishment of the mission.

c. Use of hand grenades within rock formations. All types can be effectively used at rock formations entrances, but once the team is underground the fragmentation type hand grenades are not practicable. If thrown, the effect on friend and foe alike is chaotic.

d. Use of demolition within the underground rock complex. The most effective method of underground rock complex destruction is through the utilization of demolitions. Great quantities of explosives, nearly 75 tons, were required to destroy the underground rock complexes which were found in the brigade's area of operations. Transportation of the explosives was a most difficult logistical problem. Maximum use was made of small satchel charges by tossing them into the cave entrance then exploding the charge with a claymore firing device.

e. Use of individual weapons within an underground rock complex. Due to the size of the M60 machine gun and noise it created, it was impossible to use the weapon in the caves. The identical problem exists with the M14 rifle. The XM16E1 proved to be somewhat better than either of the other two weapons due to its light weight and compact size; however, as with all weapons with high muzzle velocity, ricochets were so frequent and so dangerous that our soldiers were reluctant to use them. The best weapon by far proved to be the caliber .45 automatic pistol. As the ranges at which most kills were made were in the neighborhood of a few feet, there was little need for accuracy. The tremendous stopping power of the caliber .45 pistol at close ranges more than once literally blew the enemy down as well as killing him.

OBSERVATION:

a. The psychological effect on the enemy can be exploited by using a small portable loud-speaker encouraging the enemy to come out or be buried alive. A rock complex can be attacked through many openings by using small elements (less than fire team size) operating independently but with a common mission. Little use can be made of demolitions, or fragmentation grenades once a team is within the cave as the explosives have an equal effect on both friend and enemy. The demolitions, and fragmentation grenades affect the eardrums. Therefore, the battle within the cave rock complex returns to the most primitive of fights; man against man, using pistols at ranges of two and three feet. Here control and leadership is difficult and the will of the individual becomes the dominant factor.

b. The technique of rock complex fighting requires detailed planning and violent execution similar to the technique developed by the US Army for destruction of a fortified area. The main difference in the attack of a cave complex and the attack of a fortified area lies in the intelligence field for in a cave complex a reconnaissance is impossible.

c. Hand grenades can be employed by troops outside the caves but once inside only non-fragmentation grenades can be used, such as white phosphorous and CS, and these must be used with extreme caution. The best technique is to employ them around corners or down in crevices.

d. When underground rock complex destruction is required a great quantity of explosives will be necessary to break the vast amount of rocks that support the cave and the entrance. The transportation problem was solved by using a CH-47 helicopter with a 100 foot sling which transported the explosives directly to the rock complex entrance where the demolition was to take place. The explosives were emplaced and exploded. The technique used was to throw the small satchel charge device into the rock complex while a soldier stood by with a claymore firing device. No sooner did the charge fall to the ground than it was exploded with the firing device preventing the enemy from tampering with it.

e. Since the caliber .45 pistol has an extremely low muzzle velocity and a very heavy slug, there is little chance of a ricochet hitting the firer. The big disadvantage is the report from the pistol which at times will stun the firer, momentarily preventing a good second shot. For future operations of this nature silencers would be useful.

From *Illustrated Brochure on the Techniques for Detecting, Neutralizing and Destroying Enemy Tunnels, "Cacti Blue," 2d Battalion, 35th Infantry* (1968)

3.   VC HIDING PLACES:

a. It was found that there were three main types of holes and these were classified more by their location, than by their construction. By far the most common was the "under bamboo" hole shown in Figure 1. This hole was easily and quickly camouflaged, characteristic of all the holes found in the Due Pho–Mo Due area of Vietnam. The entrances to the holes differed widely as did the techniques of camouflage. Most of the entrances were located within the edge of a bamboo clump or just outside the edge. The hole cover or trap door contained the camouflage material. Some had pieces of cut bamboo affixed to the door itself. The edges of the door fitted snugly into the entrance. Many other entrances were covered only by the door which was camouflaged by spreading leaves, rocks, and other materials over the top. Another characteristic common to all these small tunnels was the air hole which was normally made from a hollow piece of bamboo three to four inches in diameter inserted into the tunnel and camouflaged on the surface.

b. The air hole was the only telltale indicator of the second type hole, the "beach hole." The beach hole differed from the bamboo hole in that it was made in the sand and normally constructed from cut timbers. It did not depend upon the bamboo roots to add rigidity to the roof. Naturally, the entrance to a beach hole was impossible to locate as it was often buried under a foot of loose sand; however, it could be detected by finding the breathing tubes. Some air holes were a continuation of the bamboo frames that made up the local fisherman's "lean to." Other air holes were exposed by pulling up the cacti plants that grew along the sand dunes on the

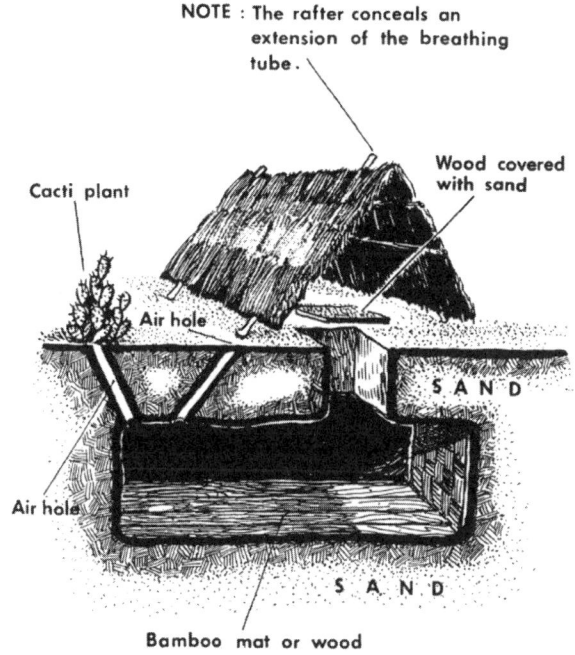

NOTE : The rafter conceals an extension of the breathing tube.

Cacti plant

Wood covered with sand

Air hole

S A N D

Air hole

S A N D

Bamboo mat or wood

Concealed Viet Cong tunnel entrance.

beach. The enemy was clever in hiding breathing tubes and the battalion was just as clever in locating them. (See Figure 2).

c. The third type of tunnel, the least common, was the "water entrance" type. This tunnel was located near a small stream or beside an old bomb crater that was filled with water. Normally, these holes had no lid and depended on the natural growth along the stream bank to hide the entrance. Sometimes the entrance was completely submerged, but not always. A typical tunnel is depicted in Figure 3.

4. <u>INDICATORS:</u>

a. No matter what type of hole faced, the slogan "find 'em – fix 'em – fight 'em and finish 'em" was as true as the day it was first promulgated; however, many units failed to put the sequence in proper order. During several of the operations, the enemy was fixed and fought only to learn that there was nothing to finish. The unmatched success of the battalion was due primarily to finding the enemy through the deliberate search technique before attempting to fix or fight. The one true indicator of success was the actual number of enemy killed or captured and the number of weapons seized. During the period of 10 July–10 August, the battalion killed 386 enemy, captured 77 POWs and seized 158 weapons while suffering only 12 US soldiers killed in action. The high kill ratio and large number of weapons captured was the result of locating the enemy within his hiding place. Once the enemy was located, the job was relatively simple as the enemy had fixed himself by choosing a small tunnel in which to hide. The enemy, dependent only on his expertise at passive camouflage, had no other choice but to be killed or captured, as defense of a small hole against an American rifle squad was difficult if not impossible. The key to a successful search was the application of common sense to the situation in Vietnam. The Battalion assigned a rifle company a small search area, never larger than a 1000 meter grid square. These small areas were picked based on intelligence reports or past actions. The company then painstakingly searched every square meter of the area. There was no time limit to complete the task. Units were able to capitalize on the natural curiosity of the American soldier in developing techniques of deliberate search. Normally, the first and foremost technique was the art of locating the hole. There are several indicators that proved to be helpful in locating these holes. Visual indicators often disclosed the general area of the hole but not its precise location. Worn places on the bamboo that the enemy had used as handholds were good visual indicators. Another indicator was a small trail, much like a game trail, through the brush into a bamboo clump. Easily seen, although not a sure sign, was cut bamboo as shown in several of the photographs. Frequently, the VC dug their holes under these partially harvested bamboo clumps. A good visual indicator, but difficult to detect was a slight depression in or around the bamboo clump. This depression was often the location of a trap door. The depression collected leaves and trash and aided in the camouflage of the hole entrance. The surest of all visual indicators was the ever present air hole. Once located, these bamboo breathing tubes revealed the tunnel below. Visual indicators were by far the best indicators but they were not the only ones. A lone individual, especially a female, signaled that the VC were not far away. She placed the finishing touches of camouflage around the holes. Fresh cooked food with no one attending the pot was a sure sign the VC departed in haste or were hidden nearby. The VC, being lazy and not very good soldiers, often disclosed their locations by disposing of human waste near their hole. Fresh human feces pointed out an unwary enemy.

b. All of these indicators were good; however, in each different area of Vietnam they may vary. Experience will tell what the indicators are within an area. Once the individual soldier achieves success at locating the enemy, he will almost be able to "smell them." There is a certain sixth sense about locating the enemy, but more often than not it is knowing where to look and what to look for. The indicators are what to look for. The places to look are in the corners of hedgerows, in the corners of villages and in the corners of trails or trenches. The enemy often hides in these corners as he can see from them while not being seen. Additionally, hiding in a corner allows the party who puts the finishing touches on the camouflage to escape undetected. The enemy is aware of the danger in establishing a pattern; however, he must have a location that provides him with observation as well as concealment, so look for an observation post that allows him to move into or out of the area undetected.

5. TECHNIQUES:

a. The techniques of deliberate search that have been successfully employed centered around the rifle squad. The squad divided into a security team and a search team. Naturally, the curious went to the search team while the less curious provided the security. Needless to say, these positions were rotated after a period of time as the thorns in the bamboo clumps damaged the hands, arms and uniforms. Each platoon assigned the squad a search area and they in turn started a systematic search along the hedgerows and bamboo clumps. Meanwhile, the security element moved toward the limits of each search area. Once a hole was discovered, the security element surrounded the area while the searchers cleared away enough brush to allow the comparatively large American soldier to operate within this confined space. Then hole reduction began.

b. Reduction of the hole was a simple four step process beginning with a soldier firing one or two magazines from his M-16 into the trap door. This had a tendency to discourage enemy grenadiers from getting too close to the door. After getting their attention with a magazine or two, various American and Vietnamese expressions were shouted into the hole exhorting the enemy to come out or be killed. Sometimes he gave up without a fight, saving not only the effort of killing him, but of excavating the tunnel for weapons and documents. When all else failed and the "Hard Core Charlie" remained within his self-created tomb a few strategically placed grenades normally reduced both the tunnel and "Charlie" to rubble leaving only the messy task of digging out the remains. Frequently the M-16 fire opened a hole large enough to allow insertion of a grenade. If not, a grenade was placed on top of the trap door or the door removed from a distance with a rope. This minimized the effects of any attached booby trap. Sometimes an air hole was enlarged and a grenade pushed through it. This was particularly effective against stubborn VC who hid behind a grenade baffle. The last step was the insertion of a tunnel rat to insure that all weapons and documents were recovered as well as all enemy killed or captured. The hole was thoroughly searched as the enemy has small compartments built into his holes to hide weapons and ammo. Obviously, it was far better to capture the VC as he could frequently lead one to another hole containing items of interest, but in any event, capture saved the time wasted digging out the hole for weapons and documents. After the hole was searched, it was destroyed with explosives if it had not already been destroyed in the four step process. A caution to remember is that the enemy's defense is to toss out a grenade when everyone is standing around the hole and attempt to escape from another exit of the tunnel. Many of these holes had two entrances so naturally the best defense against the grenade tosser was dispersion of forces and alert security men who fired into the hole before the grenade or "Charlie" came out.

c. It is apparent that the success of the operation depended entirely on the success of the searchers. Accordingly, the best men were used first. As soon as the unit found success in "Hole Huntin", everyone desired to be a searcher. But as success usually is, it was short lived and frequently the unit's enthusiasm dwindled to a low ebb. Many a bleeding hand of a Lieutenant finally located a hole that rekindled the desires of his searchers and the race was on to locate the next hole. The noncommissioned officers lead the way in the search for holes and maintained in the searchers an enthusiastic approach to the mission. This contributed materially to the successful operation.

WELL - TUNNEL COMPLEX -- BEN CAT AREA

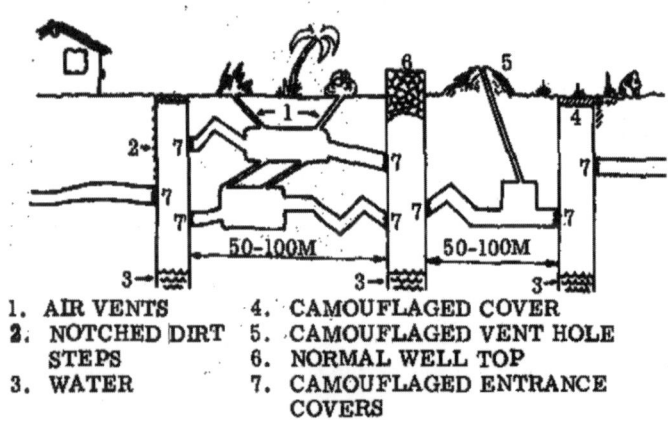

1. AIR VENTS
2. NOTCHED DIRT STEPS
3. WATER
4. CAMOUFLAGED COVER
5. CAMOUFLAGED VENT HOLE
6. NORMAL WELL TOP
7. CAMOUFLAGED ENTRANCE COVERS

A diagram of a typical Viet Cong tunnel layout.

Both the NVA and the VC had elite sapper units within their ranks. These soldiers were specialists in assaulting and breaking through American defensive perimeters, such as those around a firebase, infantry HQ, fortified hamlet, or other protected target, often using heavy weaponry such as rocket launchers, bangalore torpedoes, mines, heavy mortars, and flamethrowers. The size of the sapper units ranged from independent squads of just a handful of men through to entire battalions and regiments. The following document, produced in 1969 by the HQ of XXIV Corps, illustrates how seriously the threat from the sappers was taken, and also gives a window into U.S. defensive tactics in Vietnam.

From "Lessons Learned—Defense Against Sapper Attacks" (1969)

(1) Day and night recon patrols. Defending units should prepare and implement as extensive a patrol plan as possible. Recognizing that infantry resources at a fire base or fixed installation seldom meet the basic needs of the commander, it remains imperative that a continuous effort be made to detect the sapper during either the reconnaissance or the movement to contact. The size of the friendly recon patrol will naturally have to be based upon the enemy threat in the area. The distance the patrol travels from the fire base or installation will also be contingent upon knowledge of enemy activity. It should be emphasized, however, that friendly patrols need not necessarily operate at great distance from the base, because sapper recon elements invariably attempt to get close to the objective area, and sapper forces must be positioned within but a few hundred meters of the perimeter wire many hours before the assault begins. The mission of early detection can therefore normally be accomplished by small screening parties operating in the immediate area around the fire base or installation. In this regard, an analysis of the historical example will show that two or three small patrols conducted by friendly forces just prior to dusk along a line some 200 meters outside the wire would have uncovered the enemy force at a time when he was most vulnerable.

(2) Deception and counterintelligence. It will be noted that the sapper bases his plan of attack on detailed knowledge of defensive installations and patterns normally followed throughout the day and night. Commanders should therefore develop plans to deceive the enemy and hinder his reconnaissance. Such plans should include provisions for false bunkers and gun positions, movement of key installations from time to time, variation in patrol schedules, and the emplacement of dummy anti-intrusion devices to augment the actual devices around the perimeter. Effective deception and counterintelligence measures are products of the imagination, usually the result of thorough knowledge of sapper techniques combined with the promulgation of ever-changing ideas designed to confuse the enemy. One of the major deficiencies noted in the study of past sapper attacks was the constant use of the same locations for listening posts. An imaginative commander prepares plans for dummy listening posts as wells as for posts that are never in the same location two nights in a row.

(3)   Anti-intrusion devices. A unit programmed to occupy a fire support base or a fixed installation can never emplace enough anti-intrusion devices. Defense plans must provide for continuous improvement of those devices which exist and progressive augmentation thereof. Mines and booby traps affixed to trip wires must be carefully plotted in the interest of safety. However, the trip flare is a device which can and should be used in great numbers and in those locations where the enemy is not likely to expect them. A trip flare emplaced on high ground overlooking the defensive perimeter or on avenues of approach well away from the perimeter will cause the sapper immeasurable difficulty. He expects a pattern of wires, booby traps and trip flares in the general vicinity of the perimeter. If he discovers or trips a flare hundreds of meters from the objective area, he will be forced to proceed with even greater caution than he normally does. The principal factor in this technique involves constant and continuous improvement of the defensive position. This is a platitude all too frequently ignored because of limited personnel resources and the press of other business. Nevertheless, the commander who adheres to this principle and expands his detection devices as far as available resources will permit will seldom be subjected to the assault phase of a sapper attack.

(4)   Troop alertness. It is a known fact that the VC/NVA will wait until boredom on the part of friendly forces causes the guard to be lowered. There is little that can be said relative to the requirement to insure that listening posts and personnel on the perimeter are alert at all times. This is a command function, and it is up to the commander to develop supervisory techniques designed to motivate the men. Practice alerts and a system of continuous inspections (particularly during the early morning hours) seem to produce favorable results.

(5)   Illumination of defended area. One of the keys to an effective defense against sapper attacks is illumination. The sapper is trained to operate in the dark, and once he penetrates the perimeter wire, he relies on confusion among the defenders and their inability to differentiate between the defender and the attacker. Thus, periodic illumination (at varied intervals) will assist in the detection of approaching sappers, and continuous illumination once the assault has begun will work to the benefit of the defending forces. In many fire bases throughout the XXIV Corps area there is one 81mm mortar tube prepared at all times for immediate illumination of the objective area.

(6)   Deconstruction of the enemy after the assault has begun, If the sapper is successful in reaching the perimeter wire without being detected, he is still extremely vulnerable during that period when he is attempting to penetrate the wire. It is here that effective fire from the perimeter guards will pay the greatest dividends. As soon as any member of the perimeter detects an attempt to penetrate the wire, the area should be illuminated, and every effort should be made to destroy the enemy during the process of penetration. In this regard, extensive use of tangle foot between external and internal perimeter wires will keep the sapper in the kill zone for a longer period of time.

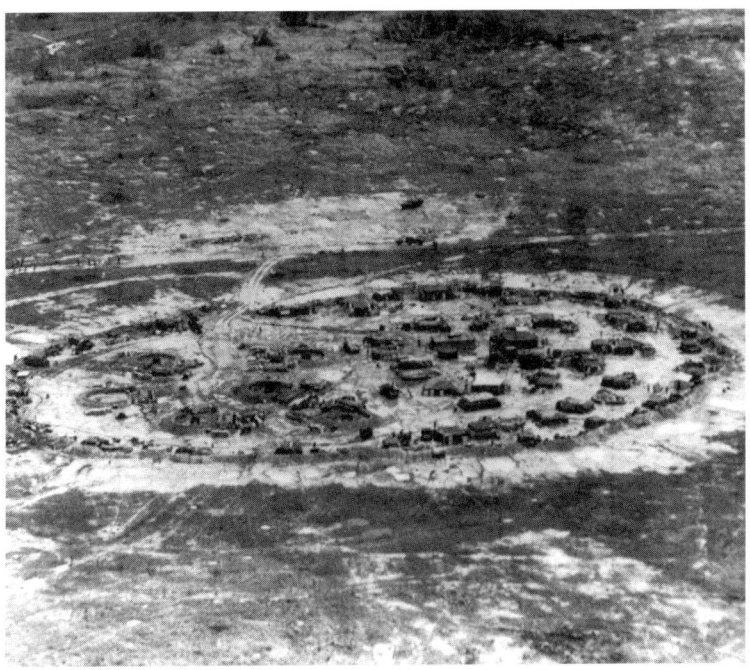

A U.S. Fire Support Base (FSB Crook), June 1969.

(7)   Use of bunkers. The bunker is the worst place to be during a sapper attack. Although a well constructed bunker can sustain a direct hit by an 82mm mortar round, the sapper is trained to fire his RPG at the apertures of the bunker, thus preventing the defender from participating in FPL [Final Protective Line] fires. It should be axiomatic that only critical bunkers (such as FDC's [Fire Direction Center] and communications bunkers) remain occupied when mortar fire begins to hit the objective, and even these bunkers should be protected by a guard stationed in a foxhole outside the installation, and another in the entrance. A well prepared foxhole in the vicinity of the bunker becomes a far more effective fighting position than the bunker itself and is less likely to be a target for crew served weapons and small arms employed by the attacking force. A soldier occupying a foxhole will not normally sustain injury from incoming mortar fire unless his position receives a direct hit.

(8)   Reaction force and internal firing. Every defensive position, regardless of how small, should have a reaction force, whose mission is to assault the enemy elements that have penetrated the wire. This force need not be particularly large.

It should, however, be capable of assembling rapidly and moving to predesignated positions within the perimeter. The reaction force should be rehearsed to insure that every man knows his job. Additionally, specified individuals in the defending force should be designated to fire at targets within the wire. Sappers pay little attention to activity of individuals within the perimeter unless those individuals are blocking their movement to their assigned objective. They can be eliminated by effective internal fire.

(9) Use of signals. Some provisions should be made to alert everyone within the perimeter, as well as listening posts outside the perimeter, of the fact that a penetration has been made. Almost all historical examples indicate that a significant percentage of the defending force was unaware of a penetration until it was too late. Signals should be simple and easy to employ by all members of the command. Visual signals, such as a red flare, are perhaps the most effective means available because of the noise and confusion that exist during the initial phases of the assault.

(10) Miscellaneous. The following additional recommended techniques should be considered by the defending commander:

(a) "Telltales" should be used extensively around the outside of the perimeter. These include the raking of sand strips so that footprints will show up and the arrangement of trees and bushes in such a manner that their disturbances by the sapper recon parties will be detected by friendly screening patrols.

(b) Units should be directed to save C ration cans and affix them to wire and bushes to serve as warning devices.

(c) Sapper attacks should be expected along the least likely avenues of approach—through swamps, blown timber, and trash dumps. Defensive positions should therefore provide for adequate observation of these avenues and the construction of additional obstacles to augment the natural ones.

(d) Within the defensive perimeter internal wire systems should be constructed (progressively, as time permits) around artillery pieces and critical installations. The ultimate objective should be a checkerboard network of internal perimeters which will force the enemy into a pocket if he succeeds in penetrating the external perimeter.

(e) Personnel stationed along the perimeter who suspect the presence of the enemy should be advised to use hand grenades and M-79 fire until such time as the enemy is definitely identified. Sapper recon parties occasionally probe a perimeter to test alertness of the defending force and locate individual firing positions.

One of the ultimate nightmares for the U.S. infantryman was to become separated from his unit and captured by an enemy known for his cruelty to prisoners. The possibility of being captured was not theoretical. On September 22, 1968, for example, Staff Sergeant Buddy Wright, a squad leader with Company D, 1st Battalion, 22d Infantry Regiment, 4th Infantry Division, was captured by a small communist force and held in a remote camp. On the fifth night of his capture, he managed to escape, and survived the next 10 days in the jungle living off the land while evading an enraged enemy, finally reaching safety. The insights from FM 21-76, *Survival, Evasion and Escape* (1969), therefore, were doubtless studied with some intensity by many infantrymen.

From FM 21-76, *Survival, Evasion and Escape* (1969)

CHAPTER 10
SHORT-RANGE EVASION

10-1. Special Aspects of Short-Range Evasion

a. Short-range evasion generally is conducted relatively near friendly areas as a result of isolation of units or individuals who are separated or lost from their parent unit.

b. The principles and aids discussed in the preceding chapter are applicable to short-range evasion.

10-2. Hazards of Isolated Units

In the past, most prisoners of war were captured when their units were isolated by enemy action. Under modern concepts of land warfare, the threat of isolation faces all round combat units.

10-3. Courses of Action

When a unit becomes isolated, some courses of action to be considered are—

a. Continue mission as originally assigned.

b. Defense of present position.

c. Breakout to areas under friendly control.

d. Evasion by exfiltration.

e. Combination of any of the above.

10-4. Defense of Present Position

The defense of your present position may be adopted when your unit occupies or can move to good defensive terrain, and early relief by friendly forces is probable.

The decision to hold or to attempt evasion rests with the next higher headquarters. If there are no communications with this headquarters, the decision is made by the senior man present.

10-5. Breakout to Areas Under Friendly Control

a. A breakout is appropriate when the enemy forces opposing an isolated unit are relatively weak. If this is the action decided upon, the breakout should be accomplished as soon as practicable. The longer aggressive action is delayed, the greater the advantage gained by the enemy.

b. A hastily conceived but aggressively executed plan may in some cases, be more desirable than a deliberate plan that is not timely. The actual breakout may be improved by taking advantage of the cover of darkness or inclement weather conditions; however, this will depend upon the situation.

[…]

10-6. Evasion by Exfiltration

The alternative to the breakout is evading by exfiltration. This may be the best solution if a breakout is impracticable. Separate into groups of not more than four men, with one man in command of each group. This size group reduces the chance of detection, improves movement and control, and increases confidence through the use of the buddy system.

10-7. Other Alternatives

a. Any other course of action taken to avoid capture is justified as long as it does not violate existing rules of warfare. You are subject to trial as a war criminal if such rules are violated; for example, if a hostage is killed who is no longer needed for the purpose of escape or evasion, or if the Red Cross emblem is misused to gain protection to which you are not entitled.

b. A combination of any of the above alternatives might, be the solution for a given situation.

10-8. Evasion Techniques

a. When evading alone, avoid panic, overcome fear and shock, and think before acting. Recall any previous briefings, SOP, or training, and choose a course of action that will help in returning to friendly territory. Assess those factors to your advantage (terrain, water, weapon, etc.), and those to your disadvantage (terrain, enemy, distance, etc.) before selecting a course of action.

b. If forced to parachute into hostile areas, decide what equipment to keep and how and where to dispose of the remainder. Presume that the enemy observed your descent. The important thing is to get away from the scene of landing as soon as possible, even at the expense of leaving material behind.

      c. Contact no one, except in the special case of trying to get in touch with assistance personnel in an E&E net.

[…]

10-9. Evasion in Stability Operations

The general nature of stability operations requires a variation of evasion techniques since there is little distinction between friendly and hostile territory. Areas that are under friendly control one day may be under the control of insurgent forces the next day.

      a. Advantages.

      (1) In this type of environment, friendly forces may provide a measure of security throughout the country. Therefore, distances to be traveled may be much shorter than in other types of warfare.

      (2) The risk involved in contacting the local population must be considered carefully. When evading with friendly indigenous personnel, contact with the natives of the country is easier. Knowledge of the environment, language, customs, ethnic groups, and peculiarities of the various locales make traveling and contact easier and more secure.

      (3) You may be oriented in relation to present position, location of friendly units, and the current tactical situation.

      b. Disadvantages.

      (1) It is difficult to distinguish the insurgent from the friendly populace. Also, since the government forces may employ a nonuniformed paramilitary force against the insurgent force, it is possible to mistake friendly personnel for insurgents and vice versa.

      (2) Little or no assistance from local "neutrals" may be expected since much of the population lives in fear of the insurgent force.

      (3) Occasionally, it is worthwhile for the insurgent force to take selected prisoners for propaganda purposes; but normally an insurgent unit cannot afford to allow prisoners to interfere with its movement. Even when they do take prisoners, the insurgent force often has never heard of, nor will it follow, the provisions of the Geneva Convention regarding the treatment of prisoners.

      (4) Since most insurgencies occur in less developed areas of the world, the majority of which are located in tropical or semi-tropical regions, survival presents problems peculiar to these conditions.

CHAPTER 5
AIRMOBILE COMBAT AND AIR/FIRE SUPPORT

The U.S. infantry fighting in Vietnam enjoyed two tactical advantages that their enemies simply could not match. The first was the unrivalled mobility offered by rotary-wing aviation (helicopters). The U.S. military had pioneered mass infantry maneuvers via helicopter during the Korean War, but it was during the 1960s that the concept of rotary tactical airlift became more formalized and scaled-up, assisted by the improvement of utility helicopter types such as the Bell UH-1 "Huey" and the Boeing HC-1 (CH-47) Chinook. Eventually, the U.S. Army's helicopter force became capable of moving entire battalions, regiments, and divisions, the latter embodied in purpose-designed formations such as the 1st Cavalry Division (Airmobile). Helicopters not only enabled infantry forces to cross terrain in minutes that on foot would take days, they also enabled the placing of troops in tactically advantageous but remote positions, wrongfooting the enemy from the outset. Armed helicopter gunships also acted as a nimble form of flying aerial artillery to support ground troops.

The second major advantage the U.S. infantry had was that it could usually draw upon massive fire-support resources. These included the aforementioned helicopter gunships, fixed-wing strike aircraft, heavy artillery, and even naval gunfire when operating along coastal areas. On many occasions, major enemy forces were prevented from overrunning infantry units once B-52s began dumping tons of ordnance in the area, Skyraiders skimmed napalm and white phosphorous bombs into the trees, and 105mm artillery shells came raining down with precision.

The following two sources—one the invaluable *Handbook for US Forces in Vietnam* and the other a "lessons learned" report—explain in detail the practicalities of rotary-wing operations and support fire. Although such firepower and resources were not in themselves enough to defeat the communists, they certainly meant that the Americans lost no battle in Vietnam.

From *Handbook for US Forces in Vietnam* (1966)

CHAPTER 4
COMBAT SUPPORT

INTRODUCTION

Tactical air support, armed helicopters, artillery, and naval gunfire have proven extremely effective against the Viet Cong. As a consequence he has learned to take full advantage of inadequacies in fire support planning and exploit the limitations placed on fire support means by bad weather or poor visibility. Thorough fire support planning and coordination is therefore imperative. A number of effective techniques for the employment of these combat support means are discussed below.

SECTION I. AIR SUPPORT

1.   General

Air power in all its forms plays a vital role in the war against the Viet Cong. Well-directed air strikes have often forced them to abandon carefully dug-in complexes. The frequent and deadly attacks by Strategic Air Command B-52 bombers have made VC installations in former safe havens vulnerable and lucrative targets. Improvements in the use of aircraft for all purposes will continue to increase the effectiveness of our air power.

2.   Tactical Air

a. Missions of Tactical Air. The primary role of tactical air in Vietnam is to provide close air Support for ground forces and to strike VC encampments and routes of reconnaissance and can provide assault airlift as required.

b. Armament Available.

(1) High explosive bombs varying from 100 to 2000 pounds are used when destruction of a target is desired.

(2) Napalm is an effective antipersonnel weapon frequently used against the VC. Although it will neither collapse nor destroy reinforced bunkers, it will usually kill the occupants.

(3) Fragmentation bombs are extremely effective against exposed personnel. Since they explode the air and shower thousands of fragments in all directions, they are excellent preassault and area suppression munitions.

(4) Air-to-surface missiles are used against fortified positions and other point targets. Thus far, only a few VC targets suitable for destruction by air-to-surface missiles have been located.

A Skyraider aircraft drops napalm over Viet Cong positions, 1967.

(5) 20mm guns installed on most tactical aircraft provide highly accurate firepower effective against a large variety of ground targets.

c. Operating Techniques.

(1) Tactical Air Control System (TACS).

(a) The tactical air control center (TACC) is located at Tan Son Nhut Air Base near Saigon, and is the combined US and VNAF facility which plans and coordinates the entire tactical air effort within Vietnam.

(b) Direct air support centers (DASC) are located with the four corps headquarters. The primary function of the DASC is to process and approve all requests for immediate and preplanned air support.

(c) Tactical air control parties (TACP) are attached to each battalion and higher level ground force The TACP separate brigade and division level consists of an air liaison officer (ALO). The TACP at battalion level consists of one forward air personnel and equipment. A FAC is attached to each province advisory team in Vietnam. This FAC advises the province chief on the use of tactical air and controls the air strikes within that province. TACPs are normally located with the unit fire support coordination center (FSCC) or tactical operations center (TOC) as appropriate. Duties of TACP personnel are as follows:

1. The ALO advises the ground force commander on air matters pertaining to the capabilities and employment of tactical air.

2. The FAC is an experienced tactical fighter pilot who has extensive knowledge of tactical air ordnance capabilities and fighter delivery techniques, and who has been specially trained to perform his primary mission of directing air strikes. Experience in Vietnam has shown that the FAC is most effective directing air strikes when he is airborne. When an ARVN Ranger Battalion in IV Corps was hit by a large VC force one night in March 1965, a FAC at province headquarters immediately requested a flareship and fighters. He proceeded to the battle area in an O-IF and established radio contact with the US advisors who were trapped in the compound. Being completely familiar with the area and having obtained the location of VC forces from the US advisors, the FAC was able to direct the fighters effectively on target. The Ranger unit, together with the Americans, took advantage of this situation and withdrew to a secure area. A reaction force sent in the next morning credited the air strike with killing 38 VC and preventing them from overrunning the post.

(2) Air Support Request Procedures.

(a) Requests for immediate air strikes may originate at any echelon and are forwarded through normal channels of communication to the battalion CP. The requests are validated by the battalion commander or his representative and given to the TACP for submission directly to corps headquarters direct air support centers (DASC). The TACPs at province, brigade and division levels monitor all requests and coordinate with the fire support coordination center (FSCC) at their level. Provided no echelon above the battalion disapproves the request, the DASC completes the necessary coordination and orders the mission. If available aircraft are in the vicinity of the target area, the response time will be a matter of minutes. If the immediate air strike mission requires the scrambling of fighters from ground alert, it may be thirty minutes before the fighter aircraft are over the target area.

(b) Preplanned requests for air support are forwarded to the DASC where they are evaluated, assigned a priority, consolidated and then incorporated into the fire support plan for the attack.

(3) Locating VC Movement at Night. Two techniques for locating VC movement at night have proven to be extremely successful. Both methods, "Snipehunt" and "Lightning Bug", employ airborne radar combined with quick reacting armed aircraft.

(a) Snipehunt. Fighter aircraft are the quick reaction fire power used in the Snipehunt. Once a target has been located by airborne radar and clearance has been obtained from the ground force commander, a flareship is called in to illuminate the target area for a FAC-controlled fighter aircraft. An example of the effectiveness of this technique was demonstrated in August 1965. The VC had just completed loading seven sampans with supplies, and started moving across the Saigon River in the middle of the night. The sampans' movement was detected airborne radar and, in a matter of minutes, airborne fighter aircraft and a flareship were summoned and all seven sampans were sunk.

(b) Lightning Bug. The Lightning Bug method employs a team of searchlight-equipped helicopters and three or four armed helicopters. After the target has been located by airborne radar and clearance obtained from the ground force commander, the helicopter team is called into action. The searchlight helicopter illuminates the target and the armed helicopters attack and destroy it. A variation of this method is the armed ship and the searchlight helicopter working as a team without the assistance of radar. Once a target is identified and illuminated, the armed ships attack and destroy it. Lightning Bug teams have been particularly successful against VC vehicular boat movements.

3. Armed Helicopters

a. Missions. Armed Helicopters can provide timely and accurate fire support in both offensive and defensive actions. They are normally employed to escort transport helicopters and deliver suppressive fires. Other missions include:

A UH-1 deploys U.S. infantry on a combat mission, July 18, 1970.

(1) Armed visual reconnaissance. The purpose of this type of mission is to obtain enemy information and to locate and destroy VC targets. Normally a minimum of two armed helicopters are utilized.

(2) Convoy escort. There are two methods of performing this mission. The first method, an O-1 type observation aircraft stays with the convoy at all times, while armed helicopters deploy by bounds as the convoy progresses. The armed ships are always within five minutes flying time of the convoy. If the convoy is ambushed, the O-1 pilot immediately scrambles the armed ships by radio and directs the initial strikes on the VC ambush force. The second method – armed helicopters flying continuous column cover – is used when an aircraft is not required because the convoy distance is short or if the danger is great.

(3) Overhead cover for ground operations. The purpose here is to allow uninterrupted movement of friendly forces by providing aerial fire support as needed. The armed ships fly at an altitude which will afford the best observation without undue risk. They assist the ground force commander by:

(a) Screening flanks, front and rear of his troop units.

(b) Advising him of likely ambush sites.

(c) Advising him of likely enemy locations so he can reconnoiter by fire with small arms, artillery or armed helicopters.

(d) Providing radio relay and control.

b. Armament. Armed helicopters may have one or more of the following weapons systems; four 7.62mm machine guns and fourteen 2.75 inch aerial rockets; two rocket pods, each carrying twenty-four 2.75 inch rockets; a nose-mounted XM-75, 40mm grenade launcher; two pod-mounted .50 caliber machine guns; two 7.62mm machine guns mounted on each side of the helicopter; and/or three wire-guided missiles mounted on each side of the helicopter.

c. Operating Techniques.

1) For the proper employment of the ships and their armament, the pilots must know:

(a) The location of friendly forces. Identify friendly unit locations by using panels, smoke, colored scarves or an easily identifiable terrain feature.

(b) The location of enemy forces. Identify positions of VC forces by giving the pilot an azimuth and distance from a known location. When identifying VC forces, exercise extreme care to avoid inflicting unnecessary noncombatant casualties.

(c) The long axis of the target. Maximum advantage should be taken of the armed helicopter weapons "beaten zone" by Identifying the long axis of the target.

(d) Friendly force movements, artillery fires and the presence or absence of tactical air support. This information allows the pilot to plan his time over the target area and his rate of ammunition expenditure.

(2) Armed helicopters can be successfully employed at night if the target is illuminated by flares, searchlights, or by moonlight. This capability has been used to counter VC night attacks on many occasions.

SECTION II. ARTILLERY SUPPORT

4.   General

The missions assigned to artillery units, the ammunition used, and the basic techniques of employment are not different in Vietnam than elsewhere in the world. Here, as in Korea, artillery accounts for a large percentage of the enemy casualties.

Instances have been discovered in which the Viet Cong have actually called off attacks on friendly installations because of their fear of artillery. There are, however, refinements in artillery techniques required by the special circumstances of the fight against the VC. For example, special attention must always be given to the reduction of casualties among noncombatants. Listed below are a number of local variations in normal artillery employment procedures which may increase the effectiveness of fire support missions.

5.   Employment Techniques

a. Positioning Artillery.

(1) Since the effectiveness of artillery fire decreases as the number of firing elements is reduced, artillery normally should not be employed in less than battery size units. Three suitable battery position layouts which may be used are the "Triangular," "Hexagonal" and "Star" formations. The advantage of such dispositions is that a good dispersion pattern is maintained regardless of the direction of fire. The large number of areas requiring artillery support may reduce the number of units which can be massed on a single target; however, each fire unit should have another fire unit within supporting range for mutual defense against ground attack. Artillery must be disposed to provide support for all deploying units at all times.

(2) Be prepared for the unexpected; never assume artillery will not be needed. The threat of a VC attack from any direction is constant. Artillery units should always be prepared to fire in any direction from the firing position.

(3) The requirement for all-around fire support necessitates a change in the normal plotting chart procedures used in the FDC. Battery positions are frequently plotted at the center of the chart and the size of the chart is increased on one or all four sides to permit maximum range measurements for the weapon being employed.

(4) Azimuth stakes should be positioned around the gun pit revetment every 800 mils to facilitate rapid change of direction and reduce the possibility of firing in the wrong direction (3200 mils out). For the same reason fire commands include the desired azimuth of fire as their second element.

(5) The VC try camp out of range of the artillery whenever possible. VC operational plans take into account range and location as well as probable time required for the artillery to respond fire requests. Frequent changes of position will add to the effectiveness and the security of artillery and disrupt VC plans.

(6) Artillery units should also be prepared for rapid movement to new areas by boats, helicopters, transport airplanes, M113s or conventional

vehicles. Helicopter air movement has the advantage of increasing the number of accessible firing positions while not requiring secure ground routes.

(7) The VC consider artillery positions prime targets for mortar and ground attack. Consistent with providing prompt fire support, defensive positions with overhead protection should be prepared and improved as time permits. The FDC and ammunition should be revetted first and the position continuously improved while occupied. Defensive positions should be destroyed upon departure, since the VC may occupy abandoned positions and attempt to prevent Our return. In most cases, artillery security requires reinforcement of artillery position area defenses with infantry.

b. Fire direction.

(1) Ground observation of artillery fire is hampered by dense vegetation, especially in the jungle areas of I and II Corps. To overcome this limitation, units should take advantage of air observers for adjustment of artillery fire. The employment of WP, smoke, or a high air burst on the first round will often assist the observer in bringing subsequent rounds rapidly on target.

(2) Ground and aerial observers can often be employed effectively as a team. The ground observer marks his position and gives directions to the aerial observer, who subsequently adjusts the fire.

155mm howitzers of the 5th Battalion, 27th Artillery Regiment, 1st Brigade, 101st Airborne Division, Vietnam.

(3) A system has been developed for rapid location of target areas using an alphabetical designation for each 1000 meter map grid square within a unit's sector responsibility. The system has been used to good advantage by some units.

c. Coordination Communication.

(1) There is a great volume of air traffic throughout Vietnam. Consequently, the ability for close, rapid coordination must be maintained with operational flight elements at all times. In addition, each unit should have an individual at the firing position watching for friendly aircraft along the gun-target line. Artillery can be safely fired over air columns the fires are closely coordinated with the flight leaders.

(2) Radio has been the primary means of communication for the artillery. Experience indicated that most artillery units are employed beyond the normal rated range their FM radios. As a result, it frequently is necessary to rely on continuous employment of FM airborne radio relays and on use of AM radio communication in order to control artillery fires.

d. Special Considerations.

(1) In addition to delivering destructive fires on the VC, artillery can be utilized to illuminate critical areas at night, to orient friendly combat forces in dense undergrowth areas, to flush VC from hidden locations, to deny him escape routes, to deceive him on avenues of attack, to interdict suspected VC positions and for numerous other missions. Harassing and Interdiction (H&I) fires based on an understanding of the current intelligence situation can be very effective in demoralizing the VC both day and night.

(2) The selection of fuze action cannot invariably be dictated by terrain, as might be expected; rather, the fuze action that actually gives the best results against each specific target must be determined and selected. For example, it had long been thought that the employment of the VT [proximity] fuze in the dense jungle areas of II Corps would be ineffective. The VC had placed numerous snipers high in the trees in this zone. VT fuze action was used successfully to attack this type of target.

(3) Aerial artillery of the Air Cavalry Division provides an added artillery support capability. One of the artillery battalions in the division is equipped completely with helicopters armed with 2.75[in] rockets, SS-11 missiles, and searchlights. Elements of the battalion are used to provide closely coordinated fires in support of air assault elements, against targets that rapidly develop on the battlefield, and for attacking moving targets. The artillery countermortar program is enhanced by placing aerial

artillery helicopters on counter mortar air alert. These airborne ships are continuously alert for mortar flashes and immediately strike known or suspected locations.

SECTION III. NAVAL GUNFIRE SUPPORT

US Navy ships operating off shore can provide fast, accurate fire support for ground forces operating in the vicinity of the coast. This support can be either direct fire, where the target is visible from the ship, or indirect fire directed by air or ground observers. Because of their mobility, ships can be used to provide fire support over a wide area with little time lost between missions. Their support should be used whenever conditions permit. Ammunition available include high explosive, white phosphorous, and illuminating rounds with mechanical time, point detonating, or VT fuzes.

6.   Requests for Naval Gunfire

Any qualified observer can originate a request for artillery. The request for naval gunfire support (NGFS) is transmitted through normal fire support channels to the nearest fire support coordination center (FSCC) where a naval gunfire liaison officer (NGLO) is located or to the nearest coastal surveillance center (CSC). The CSC or NGLO will complete processing of the request. The NGLO will also make arrangements for the necessary observers or spotters. Requests for NGFS must contain the following information:

      (1) Coordinates of target.

      (2) Target description (troops in open, caves, etc.).

      (3) Time ship is to commence firing.

      (4) Type ammunition desired.

7.   Gunfire Support

a. NGFS falls into two broad categories:

      (1) Pre-planned (requested or scheduled 48 hours or more in advance).

      (2) Nonscheduled (normally requests requiring quick response).

b. An example of the rapid reaction and accuracy of naval gunfire support occurred during the US Marine Corps operation "Starlite" in August 1965. A large group of VC attempting to cross a clearing to escape encirclement were seen by a forward observer. The grid coordinates of the clearing were radioed to the offshore ships and, within seconds, the first rounds were "on the way." When the smoke had settled, the clearing was littered with the bodies of over 60 VC.

From "Operations Report—Lessons Learned 1-68: Summary of Lessons" (1968)

5. ITEM: Utilization of gunships supporting a unit in contact. (670698)

DISCUSSION: Frequently gunships are called to an area of contact. Upon arrival on station they are then required to orbit and ultimately are never used because of the presence of other fire support means. The resolution of this problem lies in the commander's integration of the gunship support with the artillery and tactical air support available.

OBSERVATION: One solution would be to give the gunships a separate mission and area of operation within the zone of contact, such as covering the enemy's escape routes. Gunships, employed at treetop level, are particularly useful in identifying the direction and extent of enemy movement and in conducting a visual reconnaissance by fire for friendly units moving to contact.

[…]

9. ITEM: Use of armed helicopters to interdict Viet Cong escape routes, (670221)

DISCUSSION: Armed helicopters have been used successfully to observe the enemy attempting to flee operational areas during search and destroy operations. Recently it appears that the Viet Cong are trained to remain in hiding while the armed helicopters are on station and when the helicopters withdraw to rearm or refuel, to quickly withdraw from the area.

OBSERVATION: A technique successfully used is to have the armed helicopters accompany the combat assault helicopters and then orbit on station as the unit organizes and begins its search. Then at a time determined by the airmobile force commander, the gunships withdraw from the operational area and orbit in an area three to five kilometers away, and then after a five minute interval, return to the operational area at low level. This has resulted in the sighting of Viet Cong attempting to flee the area believing that the armed helicopters had been withdrawn from the area.

10. ITEM: Special considerations for night heliborne operations. (670708)

DISCUSSION: The 11th Combat Aviation Battalion reports that night combat assaults introduce two special considerations that are not present during daylight assaults. The first consideration is marking of landing zones. If the battlefield illumination is properly placed and timed, all pilots involved in the assault will know the approximate location of the landing zone. Green or yellow smoke will show up well as a mark for the desired touchdown point. If the assault is conducted without illumination, the landing zone can be marked by firing a flare pistol after the troop carriers have been vectored onto the final approach. The second special consideration for night combat assaults is notification of the troops to disembark. Troops must be cautioned to stay on the troop carriers until the aircraft commanders of each helicopter give them a signal to disembark. This is done to preclude having troops exit the helicopter prematurely while either still high above the ground or while hovering to clear obstacles such as dikes, ditches, streams or bomb craters.

OBSERVATION: Night combat assaults can be conducted on a routine basis if all the special planning considerations are evaluated. There can be no substitute for deliberate planning and professionalism.

[…]

11.   ITEM: Illumination of night heliborne operations. (670708)

DISCUSSION: The 11th Combat Aviation Battalion has participated in several night combat assaults during which several variations of battlefield illumination were used. The best means of battlefield illumination has been found to be flares, either air dropped or fired by artillery or mortars. There are two major considerations in the use of illumination. The first consideration is timing. The illumination must be properly timed during the assault to prevent compromise of the landing zone and still provide effective illumination during the landing phase. The best time to illuminate a landing zone is 2 minutes before touchdown of the assault helicopters. The second consideration is accuracy. It is absolutely essential that the flares be placed accurately. The best location for flares is on the downwind side of the landing zone on the side farthest from the fire support base in the case of mortars or artillery, or on the downwind end on one side in the case of air dropped flares. This places the illumination to the rear and to the side of the troop carriers who then are not blinded by the illumination and can use their shadows to judge height. Placing artillery and mortar flares on the side of the landing zone farthest from the fire support base provides the greatest safety factor because the projectiles pass high over the landing zone and the empty projectiles do not fall on the landing zone after ejecting the flare cannister. Dropping flares downwind of the landing zone places the illumination in the optimum location and prevents the parachute flares from becoming hazards to flight.

OBSERVATION: Battlefield illumination during night combat assaults must be carefully planned. Poorly timed or placed illumination can negate all the planning of the operation and jeopardize mission accomplishment.

12.   ITEM: Night heliborne operation without illumination. (674216)

DISCUSSION: Company A, 25th Aviation Battalion conducted a night operation, inserting troops into three landing zones without the aid of artificial illumination. Due to the nature of the mission, the ground force commander requested that no flares be dropped. The mission was accomplished in three lifts, each lift going into one false landing zone before or after dropping the troops in the actual landing zone.

OBSERVATION: On a dim night, terrain detail can be seen at altitudes above 1000 feet; however, as the flight descends toward the landing zone, terrain features will become invisible. Since the flight leader is unable to determine the distance to the landing zone, a command and control aircraft orbiting the landing zone is effective in talking the flight leader into the landing zone by furnishing altitudes and headings. The flight leader and other flight aircraft should turn on their respective search lights as they descend below 200 feet. Landing lights should be set at the proper angle while on the ground prior to departure.

[…]

14. ITEM: Landing zone clearing operation. (T674249)

DISCUSSION: Landing zone clearance for a combat assault became a matter of great concern to battalion commanders of the 1st Brigade, 101st Airborne Division during the early assaults of Operation Wheeler. Mined landing zones were frequently encountered. The landing zones were often covered by fire, both sniper and automatic weapons. The resulting casualties received when personnel leaped from the helicopters and hit anti-personnel mines had considerable effect upon the morale of men going into a combat assault and upon the time involved in moving off the landing zone. Therefore, a procedure had to be developed to insure that at least the assault troops were provided with mine-free terrain on which to land and a cleared path off the landing zone.

a. In the brigade's area of operation, most landing zone sites were obvious to the enemy; thus he had ample time to prepare the probable landing zone sites with anti-helicopter punji stakes and anti-personnel mines. In most cases, the anti-personnel mines were of the M-16 1 "Bouncing Betty" type. Since surprise is a primary advantage during combat operations, the landing zones were prepared from the air just prior to the assault. Due to the time limitations on the landing zone and the fact that the landing zones are often subject to enemy fire, engineers cannot clear a landing zone from the ground either prior to, or during, the infantry assault. This necessitated development of a fast and efficient means of clearing a landing zone or landing space for troops and pathways off the landing zone during the assault. An approach to the solution is described below.

b. The first problem solved was that of providing the helicopters with a safe place to discharge troops. To this end, the landing zone was

U.S. Army Bell UH-1D helicopters airlift members of the 2nd Battalion, 14th Infantry Regiment during Operation *Wahiawa*, a search-and-destroy mission conducted by the 25th Infantry Division, northeast of Cu Chi, South Vietnam, 1966.

prepared to receive three ships simultaneously. The "Daisy Cutter," a standard 500-pound bomb with a three foot length of pipe attached to the detonator, was developed for this purpose. The bomb explodes off the ground and clears an area approximately 20 feet in radius of punji stakes. Anti-personnel mines within nine feet of the point of detonation are exploded by sympathetic detonation. A three ship landing zone is prepared by a minimum hit on the landing zone of six 500-pound bombs and six "Daisy Cutters." This gives at least 12 locations where a ship can discharge troops safely. The next problem was to get troops off the landing zone without detonating anti-personnel mines. The solution to this problem was the M1E1 Projected Charge. This charge, weighing 92 pounds, consists of 170 feet of detonation cable which is more powerful than normal detonating cord. The cable is fired over the landing zone by means of a small rocket motor. When the cable explodes, it clears a path one foot wide and exposes any mine one foot on either side of the path. It can be prepared and detonated by two engineers in less than four minutes. To employ this method, each of the first three helicopters in the assault should carry two engineers, a Projected Charge and four infantrymen. The ships discharge the troops over a crater made by a 500-pound bomb. The engineers set up the projected charge on the lip of the crater nearest the landing zone edge, and infantrymen provide security from the crater. The charge is set and blown, producing a clearly visible path. If the landing zone is abnormally large, a series of charges should be used between craters until there is a path off the landing zone.

OBSERVATION: A landing area can be prepared with lanes for movement off the landing zone without exposing troops to mine and punji stake obstacles.

[…]

SECTION II
ARTILLERY TACTICS AND TECHNIQUES

1. ITEM: Effective use of supporting fires. (670698)

DISCUSSION: The 4th Infantry Division reported that US forces have been the most successful when they utilized artillery and tactical air fire support simultaneously. Air support should normally be used to supplement the fires of supporting artillery. The calling of a "Check Fire" to bring in tactical air is dangerous and should be limited to the immediate area/axis of the airstrike.

OBSERVATION: Units in contact should not sacrifice artillery fire for the sake of an airstrike. Both means of support should be employed to complement one another. If an airstrike is to be placed on a particular target, artillery fires may be shifted from the immediate area of the strike for its duration, but not lifted entirely. In the same manner, if artillery is being fired in support of a particular contact, tactical air should be used to block likely routes of withdrawal or to strike areas where the enemy may be assembling his reinforcements.

[…]

4 ITEM: Aerial observation. (67X071)

DISCUSSION: It is desirable that an aerial observer establish the location of all friendly troops in the vicinity of a desired target area.

OBSERVATION: The friendly units can assist an air observer by marking their positions with a readily identifiable means such as colored panels or smoke. When several friendly troop units are located near a target area, a different means of identification should be used by each unit.

5. ITEM: Methods to preclude casualties from own fires. (670826)

DISCUSSION: An observer error in judgment can result in casualties to friendly forces. Measures that can be taken to preclude errors include:

a. Warnings against making large deviation and range corrections in conjunction with changing from shell smoke or WP to HE in adjustment.

b. All friendly locations and no-fire zones should be plotted by the fire direction center on the firing chart or map.

c. Forward observers announce "DANGER CLOSE" and the direction and distance of friendly elements from the target when firing within 600 meters of friendly positions.

OBSERVATION: All units must continuously review and analyze standard operating procedures to preclude casualties from own fires.

6. ITEM: Control and adjustment of supporting fires. (670698)

DISCUSSION: The 4th Infantry Division reported that a company commander on the ground does not have the knowledge of the overall situation or the advantage of the battalion commander overhead to control the blocking fires and close air support. The most effective control of blocking fires on the enemy's avenues of approach or withdrawal and suspected areas of enemy reserves can be accomplished from the battalion commander's position in the air overhead. However, the control and adjustment of close in, direct supporting fires–200–400 meters out from the perimeter–must be left to the company commander and his artillery forward observer.

OBSERVATION: Reinforcing and blocking fires can best be controlled by a battalion commander from his command and control ship.

7. ITEM: Use of "At My Command" during fire missions. (670804)

DISCUSSION: The term "At My Command" is used by an observer during fire missions when necessary to control the time of impact due to observation or safety requirements. Many observers use "At My Command" as a common practice which can delay firing. Delays in firing after powder has been inserted will significantly increase the powder temperature causing inconsistent powder performance which can be critical during registrations.

OBSERVATION: The observer should control the fire only when observation or safety in the impact area is an over-riding factor.

[…]

27. ITEM: Artillery operations in beach and sandy areas. (670772)

DISCUSSION: The 196th Light Infantry Brigade reported that operations in beach areas, loose sand and near large bodies of water pose many considerations for a firing unit, particularly during airmobile operations. Some of these are:

a. All exposed surfaces of howitzers must be securely covered during lift and resupply due to large grains of sand being blown about.

b. Materials for constructing a platform base for the howitzer must be taken with the battery, as the displacement obtained from firing on loose sand is much too great.

c. During resupply, consideration should be given to resupply by a platoon concept; if possible, use natural obstacles, such as sand dunes, to shield one platoon from the wind effects of the resupply effort to another platoon. Firing during such resupply operations is impossible without some type of obstacle separating the platoons. Ammunition must be dropped at or very near the howitzer to prevent excessive fatigue of the men carrying ammunition in deep, loose sand.

d. Reserve or reaction forces should be assembled on high ground to facilitate their deployment.

e. Firing on loose sand causes a rippling effect of the sand which necessitates the use of some type of reinforcement for parapets. Digging in loose sand is a futile task since the sand rolls back into place.

f. The extreme temperatures encountered affect crew performance and can cause large deviations in corrections for powder temperatures. Maximum effort should be made to store all ammunition in the same manner to get the same temperature.

g. Lift capability of the CH-47 is reduced due to extreme heat and humidity. Lifts should be programmed for early morning to capitalize on the maximum lift capability of the CH-47.

OBSERVATION: Characteristics of the proposed area of operation and probable effects must always be considered during the initial planning phases.

[…]

3. ITEM: Enemy "baiting" aircraft to land in ambush area. (670607)

DISCUSSION: During a recent combat assault, a unit was airlifted into two landing zones. A short time later, an observer in an OH-23 saw several weapons lying in an open field in the general area of the landing zones but remote from the troops on the ground. Two aircraft were sent to pick up approximately 10 troops to recover the weapons. Landing in the field near the weapons, the two aircraft were brought under heavy fire. One aircraft was damaged and several casualties were incurred.

OBSERVATION: The weapons had obviously been placed as bait for an ambush. When a situation like this is encountered, artillery and air support should be used to cover friendly activities.

4. <u>ITEM</u>: Casualty evacuation by helicopter. (670801)

DISCUSSION: Due to the advent of helicopter evacuation, the casualty is often transported directly to a hospital from the battlefield. Experiences reported by the 9th Infantry Division indicate that, in many cases, it is detrimental to both the man and the mission when clearing station facilities are over-flown. The following points were emphasized:

> a. Many casualties have not been seen by medical personnel prior to pick up by dustoff and should be taken to the closest facility, such as a clearing station where resuscitative treatment is given and the patient stabilized prior to further evacuation. Further, those patients treated by the tourniquet require immediate professional medical care. The risk of Dead On Arrival is much greater when clearing stations are bypassed and additional time is spent flying to a more distant medical facility.

> b. The seriously injured and the slightly wounded are frequently placed on the same evacuation helicopter, At the clearing station the slightly wounded casualty can be treated, held for a short period and returned to duty without leaving the division area.

> c. Evacuation can be coordinated at the clearing station, thereby preventing a situation where a helicopter takes a single patient to a hospital while other patients brought to the clearing station by troop carrier helicopters or ground vehicles are awaiting evacuation.

> d. Clearing stations have the necessary equipment and professional personnel to provide resuscitative medical care and to stabilize the patient so that further evacuation will not jeopardize his health.

OBSERVATION: Whenever possible, combat operations should be supported by a clearing station in the forward support base with a medical evacuation helicopter co-located. Casualties should be brought directly to the clearing station for initial treatment and then further evacuation, if necessary.

SOURCES

CHAPTER 1

U.S. Army, FM 31-30, *Jungle Training and Operations* (Headquarters, Department of the Army, September 1965)

Department of Defense, *A Pocket Guide to Vietnam* (Department of Defense, 1962)

CHAPTER 2

U.S. Army, FM 23-9, *Rifle, 5.56-mm, XM16E1* (Headquarters, Department of the Army, July 1966)

U.S. Army, "M16 Rifle Tips" (U.S. Army, 1967)

U.S. Army, FM 23-67, *Machinegun, 7.62-mm,* M60 (Headquarters, Department of the Army, October 1964)

U.S. Army, FM 23-23, *Antipersonnel Mine M18A1 and M18 (Claymore)* (Headquarters, Department of the Army, January 1966)

U.S. Army, FM 21-15, *Care and Use of Individual Equipment* (Headquarters, Department of the Army, February 1977)

CHAPTER 3

Konrad Kellen, *A profile of the PAVN Soldier in South Vietnam*, Memorandum RM-5013-1-ISA (RAND, June 1966): 2600Micro509, Philip C. Gutzman Collection, Vietnam Center and Sam Johnson Vietnam Archive, Texas Tech University

U.S. Army, FM 31-16, *Counterguerrilla Operations* (Headquarters, Department of the Army, February 1963)

U.S. Army, "Tips on VC/NVA Booby Traps" (U.S. Army Vietnam, August 1967): 15400102015, Dana Mansfield Collection, Vietnam Center and Sam Johnson Vietnam Archive, Texas Tech University

Combined Intelligence Center Vietnam, *What the Platoon Leader Should Know About The Enemy's Jungle Tactics* (Headquarters, Military Assistance Command, Vietnam, October 1967): F015900210037, Sam Johnson Vietnam Archive Collection, Vietnam Center and Sam Johnson Vietnam Archive, Texas Tech University

CHAPTER 4

U.S. Army, FM 31-15, *Operations Against Irregular Forces* (Headquarters, Department of the Army, May 1961)

U.S. Army, FM 31-30, *Jungle Training and Operations* (Headquarters, Department of the Army, September 1965)

U.S. Army, "Annex D (Patrol Tips) to SOP No 1. 2d Bn, 35th Inf APO 96355, US Army, 1 Nov 1967" in *Standing Operating Procedures No.1, Ambush Patrols* (2nd Battalion, 35th Infantry, November 1, 1967): 23850756001, 35th Infantry Regiment Association Collection, Vietnam Center and Sam Johnson Vietnam Archive, Texas Tech University

U.S. Army, "Operations Report—Lessons Learned 1-68: Summary of Lessons" (Office of the Adjutant General, January 1968)

Major Ben G. Crosby, *Illustrated Brochure on the Techniques for Detecting, Neutralizing and Destroying Enemy Tunnels, "Cacti Blue," 2d Battalion, 35th Infantry* (Headquarters, Military Assistance Command, Vietnam, 1968)

U.S. Army, "Lessons Learned—Defense Against Sapper Attacks" (Headquarters, XXIV Corps, March 1969): F015800450121, Sam Johnson Vietnam Archive Collection, Vietnam Center and Sam Johnson Vietnam Archive, Texas Tech University

U.S. Army, FM 21-76, *Survival, Evasion and Escape* (Headquarters, Department of the Army, 1969)

CHAPTER 5

U.S. Army, *Handbook for US Forces in Vietnam* (Headquarters, Department of the Army, March 1966)

U.S. Army, "Operations Report—Lessons Learned 1-68: Summary of Lessons" (Office of the Adjutant General, January 1968): 1070804001, Glenn Helm Collection, Vietnam Center and Sam Johnson Vietnam Archive, Texas Tech University